THE M & E HANDBOOK SERIES

Basic Law
An Introduction for Students

L B Curzon
Barrister

SECOND EDITION

'Where laws end, tyrannies begin'
William Pitt

Pitman Publishing
128 Long Acre, London WC2E 9AN

A Division of Longman Group UK Limited

First published 1978
Second edition 1985
Reprinted 1986, 1988, 1989

© Macdonald & Evans Ltd 1978
© Longman Group UK Ltd 1985

British Library Cataloguing in Publication Data

Curson, L. B.
   Basic law: an introduction for students. –
   2nd ed. – (The M & E handbook series, ISSN
   0265–8828)
   1. Law–England
   I. Title
   344.2   KD661

ISBN 0-7121-0655-3

Founding Editor: P. W. D. Redmond

Printed and bound in Great Britain by
Richard Clay Ltd, Bungay, Suffolk

Preface to the Second Edition

This HANDBOOK is intended for students and general readers who, having little or no knowledge of the elements of English law, wish to understand its fundamental principles and procedures. The author has kept in mind some of the syllabus requirements of first examinations in English law, but has taken into account also the needs of readers who have a general interest in obtaining an overview of our legal system, its purpose and structure. The number of case references has been increased for this second edition and it is hoped that students will use this material as an introduction to the vast store of cases in which so much of our law is recorded. Where reference is made to statutes, the reader is recommended to examine the appropriate Acts and sections.

In this edition, the chapter content has been brought up to date and recent developments have been noted.

For those students who intend to use this HANDBOOK in preparation for a first examination, or as a swift method of pre-examination revision, the following methodical approach is recommended for consideration.

(*a*) Read through the book in its entirety, but omit the progress tests.

(*b*) Read through each chapter in detail. Move to the next chapter only after completing the progress test and checking the answers.

(*c*) Re-read each chapter swiftly, noting, in particular, general principles.

(*d*) Finally, when all progress tests have been completed and checked, attempt, at three separate sittings, under examination conditions, the test papers which form Appendix II.

I wish to thank Her Majesty's Stationery Office for permission to reproduce the Act of Parliament which appears on pp. 38–9.

1985   L.B.C.

Contents

Table of Statutes

Table of Cases

CHAPTER I

Law and Justice

INTRODUCTORY MATTERS

1. Purpose of the book. This book is intended to provide an elementary introduction to English law for those who have little or no knowledge of the subject-matter. It is in no sense a detailed account of the workings of the law; rather it is a very general overview of the basis and functioning of the English legal system. It aims at presenting to the reader some of the fundamental concepts upon which that system rests and some of the ways in which those concepts are translated into the everyday working of our system of law. Specifically, after studying the text carefully and working through the progress tests and test papers, the reader should be in a position:

(*a*) to evaluate the most important of the basic ideas underlying our legal system;

(*b*) to understand the unifying notions of "law" and "justice" which are the very keystones of our legal system;

(*c*) to outline the essential patterns of civil and criminal proceedings;

(*d*) to describe the rudiments of the criminal law;

(*e*) to sketch the outlines of some important sections of the civil law;

(*f*) to comment with understanding on the place of English law in the wider setting of our way of life.

2. Plan of the book. In order that the objectives set out above might be attained, the text concentrates on the following selected topics:

(*a*) Chapters I–IV deal with some of the theoretical bases of our law. What is meant by "law" and by "justice"? What place do they occupy in our society? Why are they indispensable to our way of life? From whence is our law derived? What characteristics give our law its unique quality? Why do everyday words, such as "possession" and "person", have highly-specialised meanings in our law?

(*b*) Chapters V–VI comment on the basis and significance of the British Constitution. The workings of Parliament are also examined. If our constitution has not been reduced to writing, can it be said to "exist"? Is the "rule of law" essential in our society? Is Parliament "supreme"? How does a Bill become an Act? What is the role of the Queen in the legislative process?

(*c*) Chapters VII–XI are concerned with the machinery and procedures of the law, with the courts and their personnel, with the conduct of civil and criminal trials, with the formalities of evidence and with appeals. What is the hierarchy of our courts? How does the House of Lords function as the final court of appeal? How are judges appointed? What is the precise difference between barristers and solicitors? Is hearsay evidence ever admissible? How are appeals from Commonwealth courts considered in the English courts?

(*d*) Chapters XII–XIV examine some aspects of our criminal law by reference to some specific types of offence. What is a crime? Is it an offence to attempt to commit a crime? Are there different categories of homicide? How does the law define assault and theft? What are some of the main offences relating to the misuse of drugs?

(*e*) Chapters XV–XVII identify and describe some of the more important facets of the many-sided civil law, by referring to contracts, torts, land law and trusts. When will the courts uphold an agreement? When does the negligence of one person become the basis of an action in tort by another? What is defamation? What are the rights of a mortgagor? What are a trustee's duties?

(*f*) Chapters XVIII–XX consider aspects of the law relating to the family, employment and consumers. What is the sole ground for divorce? Have illegitimate persons the full rights of a legitimate person? Must the signing of a will be witnessed? What is unfair dismissal? How does the law define a trade description?

3. The vocabulary of the law: a caution. One of the most important problems confronting a law student arises from the highly-specialised vocabulary which is used. It is crucial, therefore, that the student and general reader should differentiate very carefully between the everyday use of some words and their use in a restricted, technical sense in the vocabulary of the law. This is not surprising; every body of specialised knowledge has its own jargon to describe in "shorthand terms" the matters with which it is concerned. Terms such as "energy" and "heat" are used by the physicist in a very precise and unique fashion. The specialised vocabulary of the law must be approached in the light of the following observations:

(*a*) Legal terminology is often ancient in derivation; it carries the very fingerprints of English history. "Murder", "mortgage", "justice of the peace" are terms which originated many centuries ago. Anglo-Saxon and Norman concepts are reflected today in the lawyer's vocabulary.

(*b*) Legal vocabulary makes use of many Latin terms. For example, *mens rea* (*see* XII, **7**); *res gestae* (*see* X, **25**).

(*c*) Some legal phrases involve words having no parallel whatsoever with those words used in non-legal senses; they can rarely be understood by noting their non-legal use. For example, "battery" (*see* XIII, **15**); "fee simple absolute in possession" (*see* XVII, **6**).

(*d*) Legal terms may change in meaning. Thus, "burglary" has altered in meaning following the Theft Act 1968, s.9.

(*e*) Some legal terms may become obsolete. "Larceny" and "embezzlement", for example, have now disappeared from current legal usage.

(*f*) Legal idiom is often rich in social and historical overtones. Reference to a law dictionary repays exploration of the derivation of legal terms.

THE NECESSITY FOR LAW

4. Preliminary matters. Readers who have lived in developed countries in which law is a fact of everyday life may learn with surprise of the philosophical and political school of thought which denies the need for law. (This opinion must be separated from the argument—voiced even by some lawyers—which holds that there is *too much* law. This is a separate issue.) It is suggested that persons could live in society without the restraints imposed by law. Most people, however, would agree, if questioned, with the belief that, in the absence of law, man's life would be "brutish, nasty and short".

5. Civilisation and the law. It has been said that law is like the air around us: without it we would perish; often we fail to notice it until its diminution draws attention to its vital nature. The "law of the jungle"—the antithesis of civilisation—is based on the domination of the weak by the strong. Consider some earlier epochs in our history in which slavery and an absence of rights for large numbers of people were common, so that St. Augustine was able to comment with truth: "Justice being taken away, then what are Kingdoms but great robberies?"

(*a*) Our way of life, based on ownership of property, respect for the rights of others, would not endure if legal rules were continually disobeyed. Thus, the flow of road traffic involves acceptance of many rules and regulations; trade would collapse if contracts were generally ignored; ownership of property would not long survive the widespread rejection of the law relating to stealing. Civilisation, it has been suggested, reflects the acceptance of rights and duties, and these require the support of law. What is the value of the right to enjoy one's property if there is no law to enforce that right?

(b) The codes of conduct which are at the basis of civilisation have emerged from eras in which disputes were settled by blood feud and an appeal to arms. In the absence of accepted codes of procedure relating to the settling of disputes by arbitration and adjudication, there is little doubt of a return to the private warfare which characterised the darkest, lawless epochs of our history.

6. Freedom and the law. "We must all be servants of the law if we are to be free." Cicero's paradox reminds us that unrestricted freedom means no freedom. Freedom to exchange one's money for another's goods is diminished if some persons are free to counterfeit money so that it becomes worthless. Freedom to enjoy one's reputation is vitiated if one can be defamed with impunity. Freedom to live in one's home is lost if others are free to invade and occupy one's property.

(a) The existence of the law is a partial and necessary guarantee of one's rights to enjoy certain freedoms.

(b) The law discourages and punishes the disregard of rights.

(c) The law provides no more than a framework within which freedom may be realised and enjoyed; but that framework is essential to a free society.

7. Law in a changing society. Law mirrors and reflects the society of which it is a part. Our land law, for example, mirrors the lingering remnants of feudal concepts; our criminal law has reflected changes in society's attitudes to what is right and wrong. Where the law fails to bow to the winds of change it tends to fall into disrepute. The disappearance of capital punishment (save in relation to treason and piracy with violence), the many recent changes in laws affecting the rights of the consumer and the duties of the seller of goods, show some of the changes in attitudes and patterns of thought prevalent in contemporary society.

DEFINING THE LAW

8. Preliminary matters. Definitions should assist understanding. In this section we consider some of the problems involved in defining "the law" and give examples of some well-known definitions.

9. Some problems of definition. It is relatively simple to define "table" or "book", but it is more difficult to define "a well-designed table" or "a good book". No definition of "law" can be exact, since "law" is not objective, in the sense which applies to a table or book. There are many conflicting definitions of law, reflecting the attitudes of those who view the functions of the law in different ways. Two points are of importance:

(*a*) A country's "law" is not the same as its "laws". The latter term refers to statutes and other enactments, e.g. Theft Act 1968, Telecommunications Act 1984; the former term refers to the wider concepts which frame the making of laws or the very philosophy from which statutes are derived.

(*b*) The term "law" bears no relationship to "law of nature". Thus, the law of gravity posits a relationship between objects and the earth which is true at all times and everywhere in our world. The "law of contract" has no such meaning; it applies solely to the U.K. and, unlike a scientific law, can be modified or annulled by the courts or Parliament.

10. Some definitions of law. No one definition is authoritative. The following definitions are worthy of careful consideration and analysis:

(*a*) "What officials do about disputes is the law itself": Llewellyn.

(*b*) "The whole reservoir of rules on which judges draw for their decisions": Gluckman.

(*c*) "Law, in its most general and comprehensive sense, signifies a rule of action ... it is that rule of action which is prescribed by some superior and which the inferior is bound to obey": Blackstone.

(*d*) "The body of principles recognised and applied by the state in the administration of justice": Salmond.

(*e*) "The collective term for the rules of conduct for men living in a legal order": Wortley.

11. Primary and secondary rules. The "primary rules" of the law have been defined as those rules which formulate the modes in which the citizens of a state are obliged to behave. The "secondary rules" have been defined as those rules specifying the appropriate sanctions to be imposed on those who violate the primary rules, and the circumstances in which the sanctions may be applied.

JUSTICE AND LAW

12. Preliminary matters. One writer has observed, cynically: "The last place in which I would look for justice is a court of law." At the other end of the spectrum of argument is the assertion that "justice and law are synonymous". In this section we consider this matter and enumerate some well-known definitions of justice.

13. Is "justice" synonymous with "law"? Many people would agree that "justice is what the law is supposed to produce", or, conversely, that "the law is the practice of justice". Yet the existence of a gap is often admitted. A judge, in sentencing a convicted person, may express his regrets at being unable to impose a heavier sentence than that permitted by statute; he here acknowledges a gap between law and justice. The rigid application of a law, with no consideration for circumstance, may result in injustice. The rise of equity (*see* II, **9**) testifies to the fact that, in practice, "justice" and "law" may not be synonymous.

14. Definitions of "justice". "Justice" is as difficult to define as "law". The definitions given below have highly subjective overtones:

(*a*) "Justice is the constant and perpetual will to render to everyone that to which he is entitled": Justinian.

(*b*) "Justice is the correct application of a law, as opposed to arbitrariness": Ross.

(*c*) "Justice among men involves an impartial and fearless act of choosing a solution for a dispute within a legal order, having regard to the human rights which that order protects": Wortley.

15. Justice, the law and society: a reminder. The following quotations should serve to underline the importance of justice in an understanding of basic law:

(*a*) "The guiding principle of a judge in deciding cases is to do justice; that is, justice according to law, but still justice. I have not found any satisfactory definition of justice ... what is just in any particular case is what appears to be just to the just man, in the same way as what is reasonable appears to be reasonable to the reasonable man": Lord Wright.

(*b*) "Justice has always weighted the scales solely in favour of the weak and the persecuted. A just decision is a decision based on grounds which appeal to a disinterested person; it is a decision which is rendered by a person who is not involved in the conflict of interests, or which, even though it be rendered by a person involved in the conflict, nevertheless is such as a disinterested person would render or approve of": Ehrlich.

(*c*) "Conceptions of justice may vary from age to age ... It is indeed the attainment of equality, not the preserving of inequality, that modern moral and legal philosophy treat as the vital function of justice": Lord Lloyd.

PROGRESS TEST 1

1. In what sense is the vocabulary of the law said to be specialised?
(3)

2. Give some examples of terms which have a specialised meaning in law. **(3)**

3. How does civilisation depend on the existence of law? **(5)**

4. What is the relationship between freedom and law? **(6)**

5. In what sense does law mirror society? **(7)**

6. Why is it difficult to define "law"? **(9)**

7. How is the word "law" used differently in "the law of contract" and "the law of heat exchange"? **(9)**

8. Give a definition of law. **(10)**

9. What are the "primary rules" of law? **(11)**

10. Is "justice" the same as "law"? **(13)**

11. Give a definition of justice. **(14)**

CHAPTER II

The Sources of English Law

INTRODUCTORY MATTERS

1. The meaning of "sources". The term "source" has been used in relation to law in a variety of ways, for example, to refer to the formal derivation of the law (e.g. "the will of the state is the law's formal source"); or to refer to the "material origin" of the law (e.g. "Parliament is the source of much of our law"). It is the latter meaning which is used in this chapter.

2. The broad river and its tributaries. Our law has been compared with many things: with a patchwork quilt put together by the many hands of succeeding generations; with a house on to which succeeding masons have erected storey after storey. A more suitable comparison is that of a river fed by large and small tributaries, some of which have disappeared. The river may present to an untrained observer an appearance of tranquillity; yet, to the trained observer, beneath the surface may be discerned motion and, often, turbulence. Occasionally the river presents a majestic sweep; on other occasions it seems no more than a small backwater. So it is with the changing composition of English law.

3. The sources enumerated. The following important sources of English law are mentioned below:

    (*a*) common law (*see* **5–7** below);
    (*b*) equity (*see* **8–10** below);
    (*c*) Law Merchant (*see* **11–13** below);
    (*d*) legislation (*see* **14–16** below);
    (*e*) precedent (*see* **17–19** below);
    (*f*) custom (*see* **20–22** below);
    (*g*) canon law (*see* **23–25** below);
    (*h*) books of authority (*see* **26–27** below);
    (*i*) European law (*see* **28–30** below).

4. The question of Roman law. The Romans were in Great Britain for four centuries and during that time Roman law was the basis of the system of government in this country. Yet that law did not outlast the invaders. Roman law remains, today, the basis of the so-called "civil law" systems in many continental countries; it has left little mark here. The movement, at the time of the Renaissance, for its adoption in place of native law based on custom (and known as "the Reception") was strong on the Continent and in Scotland, but it had no success in England. There are a few traces of Roman law today in our system, e.g. in canon law and in the modern law relating to easements (*see* XVII, **9**). For references to Roman law in leading cases, see the judgments of Blackburn J. in *Taylor* v. *Caldwell* (1863) and of Lord Blackburn in *Dalton* v. *Angus* (1881).

NOTE: We refer today to "English" law; there is no "British" law as such.

THE COMMON LAW

5. Preliminary matters. The term "common law" is used in a variety of senses, e.g. the law "common" to England and Wales, the law resulting from judicial decisions in contrast to that made by Parliament, the law which stood in contrast to equity (*see* **8** below), and English law in contrast to continental law and its Roman basis.

6. Definition and growth of the common law. We may define the common law as "the body of law judicially evolved from the general custom of the realm".

(*a*) The important constituents of our common law were, originally, rules based on Anglo-Saxon concepts and protected by the early courts, together with customary law based on rights established by long use and general consent.

(*b*) Common law is considered as evolving, or unfolding, as judges declare, or "reveal", that which "has always been" the law.

(*c*) Norman customs shaped the early common law in accordance with some feudal forms.

(*d*) The common law survived disputes with the alternative system of equity (*see* **9** below) and is now recognised as a fundamental feature of the basis of our law.

7. Place of common law in our legal system. The reputation of common law is epitomised in Blackstone's comment that it is "the chief cornerstone of the laws of England". Its binding power rests on long and immemorial usage and "universal reception throughout the kingdom". No longer considered, in Coke's words, "the perfection of reason", it remains, nevertheless, the primary historical source of English law.

EQUITY

8. Preliminary matters. The term "equity" has several meanings in law, for example, impartiality in the hearing and resolving of a dispute. Maine defined it as: "Any body of rules existing by the side of the original civil law, founded on distinct principles and claiming incidentally to supersede the civil law in virtue of a superior sanctity inherent in those principles."

9. Definition and growth of equity. We may define equity in English law as a system of doctrines and procedures which developed side by side with the common law and statute law in its attempts to remedy some defects of common law. It developed *from* the common law and grew as a reaction *against* it; it has now, to some extent, fused with the common law as far as procedure is concerned (*see* **10** below). *See* the comments of Lord Diplock in *United Scientific Holdings Ltd.* v. *Burnley BC* (1978).

(*a*) Equity grew from the residuary jurisdiction of the kings, whose chancellors were empowered to consider appeals against the rigidity and injustices of the common law.

(*b*) As the equitable jurisdiction of the chancellors grew in significance, opposition from the common lawyers, incensed at the appearance of an alternative to the common law, mounted and culminated in James I's decision in favour of equity in the celebrated case of the *Earl of Oxford* (1615).

(*c*) Note the Supreme Court Act 1981, s. 49: "... Wherever there is any conflict or variance between the rules of equity and the rules of common law ... the rules of equity shall prevail."

10. The place of equity in our legal system. The fusion of the administration of equity and common law has not led to a fusion of their substantive rules; they remain, jointly, a vital source of a developing English law. ("The two streams of jurisdiction, though they run in the same channel, run side by side and do not mingle their waters.") Some of the maxims of equity, which enshrine basic legal principles, are: "Equity follows the law" (*see Hopkins* v. *Hopkins* (1739)); "Delay defeats equities" (*see Smith* v. *Clay* (1767)); "He who seeks equity must do equity" (*see Lodge* v. *National Union Investment Co.* (1907)); "Equity looks to the intent rather than the form" (*see Parkin* v. *Thorold* (1852)).

LAW MERCHANT

11. Preliminary matters. Law Merchant, upon which our commercial law is, in part, founded derives from the practices of the merchant community. It was, in essence, a "gloss" on the common law and was concerned with trading customs, maritime practice, local regulations relating to markets and fairs, etc.

12. Definition and development of the Law Merchant. The Law Merchant "is neither more nor less than the usages of merchants and traders ... ratified by the decisions of courts of law which, upon such usages being proved before them, have adopted them as settled law", *per* Cockburn C.J. in *Goodwin* v. *Robarts* (1875).

(*a*) It developed as trade, internal and external, produced contacts with customs and legal principles often absent from our common law practices.

(*b*) Its development resulted in the growth of local courts, such as the Courts of the Staple, some of which continued until the changed conditions of the nineteenth century.

(*c*) Many customs recognised by the Law Merchant were assimilated into the common law in the eighteenth century as a result of the work of Chief Justices Holt and Mansfield.

13. Place of Law Merchant in our legal system. The historical role of Law Merchant as a source of English law is visible in the existing law of agency, insurance and, above all, negotiable instruments. Specifically, the important Bills of Exchange Act 1882, the Partnership Act 1890 and the Sale of Goods Act 1979, have an important primary source of principle in *lex mercatoria*—Law Merchant.

LEGISLATION

14. Preliminary matters. Legislation is law-making by the sovereign power in the state, which, in the case of the U.K., is the Queen in Parliament. This topic is discussed further in VI. As a primary source of English law, legislation by Act of Parliament is of fundamental importance. In a sense, it is the hallmark of Parliamentary democracy in our country.

15. Definition and development of legislation. Legislation may be defined as "the declaration of legal rules by a sovereign legislator".

(*a*) In early times it took the form of charters, provisions, ordinances and (later) statutes.

(*b*) Its growth as a source of law is a reflection of the growth of the powers of Parliament, which, today, possesses unlimited legislative power.

(*c*) No court may go behind statute. In *British Railways Board* v. *Pickin* (1974) the House of Lords held that the courts have no power to disregard a statute and that, further, they lack power to examine proceedings in Parliament in order to determine whether or not the passing of an Act had been obtained by irregularity or fraud.

16. Place of legislation in our legal system. Legislation today takes three forms: Acts of Parliament; delegated legislation; autonomic legislation. (These are discussed in VI.) Parliament alone may legislate; Parliament alone may modify or repeal existing legislation.

PRECEDENT

17. Preliminary matters. Under the doctrine of binding precedent, a judge may be obliged to apply previous decisions of the courts to later cases (*see* VII, **26–27**). The existence of a hierarchy of courts (*see* VII) is essential for the doctrine to operate. Further, accurately recorded judgments are also essential. The advantages of precedent have been stated as "precision, flexibility and certainty". The disadvantages are rigidity and the difficulty of determining exact rules of law from a study of decided cases.

18. Definition and development of precedent. Precedent may be defined as the procedure whereby judgments or decisions are utilised so as to justify decisions in later and basically similar cases. An authoritative precedent (e.g. a decisions of the House of Lords) is generally binding; a persuasive precedent (e.g. advice of the Judicial Committee of the Privy Council) need not be followed.

(*a*) Precedent developed along with the growth of a centralised system of law and the expansion of law reporting.

(*b*) The development of the judiciary and, in particular, the growth of links within the hierarchy of the courts, allowed the development of general principles, e.g. that superior courts are empowered to *reverse* (i.e. overturn) the decisions of lower courts or to *overrule* them (i.e. overturn a statement of principle). In these circumstances, the doctrine of binding precedents grew in significance.

19. Place of precedent in our legal system. Precedent is an extremely important source of English law. The importance of reported decisions is reflected in the common law theory that precedent is merely "declaratory", but does not "make" law. "A judicial precedent speaks in England with authority: it is not merely evidence of the law but a source of it, and the courts are bound to follow the law that is so established": Salmond.

NOTE: The significant part of a reported decision is known as the *ratio decidendi* (the reason for a decision). This is, in essence, the principle upon which a case has been determined. It should be differentiated from *obiter dicta* (sayings by the way), i.e. a statement of law based on facts as found, but not forming the basis of the decision.

CUSTOM

20. Preliminary matters. Blackstone speaks of "general and immemorial custom ... from time to time declared in the decisions of courts of justice". He distinguishes, as an important historical source of our common law, three kinds of custom:

(*a*) *general customs* (the universal rule of the whole kingdom, forming the common law in its strict sense);

(*b*) *particular customs* (affecting only particular parts of the realm);

(*c*) *certain particular laws* (by custom adapted and used by particular courts).

21. Definition and development of custom. Custom may be defined as modes of conduct accepted, in the absence of their basis in declared authority, as in some way binding.

(*a*) During the early period of common law growth, custom was of considerable significance. The ancient communal courts often acted on the basis of customary law and their sanctions were derived from custom.

(*b*) The feudal courts utilised custom to develop a rigid system based on feudal relationships.

(*c*) Custom gave way later to judicial precedent (*see* **17** above) and legislation (*see* **14** above) as the law developed.

22. Place of custom in our legal system. Today, in order that a practice might be considered to be a valid custom, it must, in general, satisfy the following criteria: it must have been exercised so long "that the memory of man runneth not to the contrary"; it must have been exercised continuously and observed as of right; it must be reasonable and be contrary neither to common nor statute law; it must be regarded as having obligatory force and should not be inconsistent with other customs. *See Mills* v. *Mayor of Colchester* (1867); *North and South Trust Co.* v. *Berkeley* (1971).

CANON LAW

23. Preliminaries. The influence on the development of English law of the early law of the Catholic church has been significant. In particular, it affected the attitude of the early courts to matters such as responsibility, punishment, etc. Because the early chancellors were often clerics, it may have influenced the growth of equitable concepts. In the ecclesiastical courts it was a principal source of law.

24. Definition and development of canon law. Canon law was that law based on the codified system of Rome. It had been administered in the early "Courts Christian", founded by William I, and was applied to offences against doctrine and morality and, in some cases, to the administration of the estates of deceased persons. In the twelfth century the English bishops were obliged to accept restrictions on the jurisdiction of the ecclesiastical courts. Clashes with common lawyers culminated in the confining of ecclesiastical courts to matters affecting members of the church as such. *See*, e.g., Matrimonial Causes Act 1857; Court of Probate Act 1857.

25. Place of canon law in our legal system. Canon law remains a source of the principles of jurisdiction in the ecclesiastical courts; its influence on the development of the law relating to matrimony and probate has declined, but it has left its mark on the growth of legal doctrines relating to the formalities of marriage, in particular.

BOOKS OF AUTHORITY

26. Preliminary matters. The writings of jurists have played a very important role in the development of civil law systems; in English law, textbooks have had a less significant role. But the more authoritative textbooks remain a source of development of our law.

27. Some principal books of authority in English law. Included among the writers whose texts have acted as sources of law are: Glanvill, whose *Tractate* concerning the laws and customs of England was written in the twelfth century (*see Warner* v. *Sampson* (1959)); Bracton, whose book *Laws and Customs of England* was written in the thirteenth century (*see Coggs* v. *Bernard* (1703)); Coke, whose *Institutes* were compiled in the seventeenth century (*see Reid* v. *Police Commissioner of the Metropolis* (1973)); Blackstone, whose *Commentaries on the Laws of England* were published in the eighteenth century ("It is too late, in 1935, to show that Blackstone was wrong": *per* Humphreys J. in *R.* v. *Sandbach* (1935)). Other authors whose works are cited include Hale, Hawkins and Foster. Contemporary writers whose works are referred to in the courts include Cheshire (*Modern Law of Real Property*) and Smith and Hogan (*Criminal Law*).

EUROPEAN LAW

28. Preliminary matters. The U.K. has been a member of the European Community since 1st January 1973. The European Communities Act 1972, s. 2(1) states: "All such rights powers, liabilities, obligations and restrictions from time to time created or arising by or under the Treaties, and all such remedies and procedures from time to time provided for by or under the Treaties, as in accordance with the Treaties are without further enactment to be given legal effect or used in the United Kingdom shall be recognised and available in law, and be enforced, allowed and followed accordingly...."

29. Community law as a source of English law. Community law may appear in English law in the form of the Treaties themselves, or in the form of *regulations* (which have general application and are binding in their entirety on all member states); *directives* (which are binding only as to the result to be achieved on member states); *decisions* (which bind only those to whom they are addressed). The *recommendations and opinions* of the Community have no binding force.

30. Place of Community law in our legal system. English courts must take judicial notice (*see* X, **16**) of decisions of the European Court of Justice on questions as to the meaning of the Treaties: European Communities Act 1972, s. 3(2). "... When we come to matters with a European element the Treaty is like an incoming tide. It flows into the estuaries and up the rivers. It cannot be held back.... In the task of interpreting the Treaty, the English judges are no longer the final authority.... The supreme tribunal for interpreting the Treaty is the European Court of Justice, at Luxembourg": *per* Lord Denning in *H. P. Bulmer Ltd.* v. *J. Bollinger S. A.* (1974). *See* also *Macarthys Ltd.* v. *Smith* (1981); *R.* v. *Goldstein* (1983); VII, **19**.

THE PROBLEM OF LAW REFORM

31. Preliminary matters. The law must not remain static and machinery is needed for examining proposals for reform. Parliament may set up Royal Commissions or Commissions of Inquiry. Other bodies concerned with law reform are mentioned below.

32. Law Commission. Following the Law Commissions Act 1965, a body of five commissioners and consultants was set up to keep under review "all the law with which they are concerned with a view to its systematic development and reform, including in particular the codification of such law, the elimination of anomalies, the repeal of obsolete and unnecessary enactments, the reduction of the number of separate enactments and generally the simplification and modernisation of the law".

33. Criminal Law Revision Committee. Established in 1959, this body advises the Home Secretary on aspects of the criminal law of England and Wales and makes recommendations in the form of reports. Thus, the important Theft Act 1968 arose from the committee's report on theft and related offences.

PROGRESS TEST 2

1. What is meant by a "source of law"? **(1)**
2. Enumerate the principal sources of English law. **(3)**
3. What is meant by the term "common law"? **(5)**
4. What is the place of equity in our legal system? **(10)**
5. Explain the nature of the Law Merchant. **(12)**
6. What is meant by "legislation"? **(15)**
7. How important is precedent as a source of law? **(19**)
8. What criteria must be satisfied if a practice is to be considered as a valid custom? **(22)**
9. Is canon law of significance today in our legal system? **(25)**
10. Enumerate some of the principal textbooks of authority in English law. **(27)**
11. In what sense is European Community law a part of our legal system? **(30)**
12. How is law reform reviewed in the U.K.? **(32, 33)**

CHAPTER III

Classifications and Characteristics of English Law

INTRODUCTORY MATTERS

1. Object of classification. Classification enables us to note and examine the relationships among the hierarchy of the types of law. There is no unique, authoritative classification; those set out in Fig. 1 are adopted for purposes of simplification.

2. Significance of the characteristics of English law. By "characteristics" is meant those distinctive features of English law which, in sum, differentiate it from other legal systems. They stem principally from the historical, social and political contexts within which English law has grown. To a large extent, they reflect the nature of a democracy.

SOME GENERAL CLASSIFICATIONS OF LAW

3. Basic classifications. *See* Fig. 1. Law may be classified thus:

(*a*) *International law.* This is based on those agreements entered into by nations among themselves, resulting in a corpus of legal rules applying among sovereign states.

(*b*) *Municipal law.* This is the law of a single, sovereign nation or state.

4. Further classification. *See* Fig. 1. Municipal law may be further classified, thus:

(*a*) *Common law and statute law.* This classification is based on:

(*i*) *common law*, based on custom, precedent, etc.;

(*ii*) *statute law*, based on law resulting from Acts of Parliament.

(*b*) *Common law and equity.* This classification is based on historical development. *See* II, **5, 8**.

(*c*) *Private law and public law.* This classification is based on:

(*i*) *private law*, which includes those branches of law concerned with the claims of individuals against one another, e.g. law of contract;

(*ii*) *public law*, which includes those branches of law reflecting

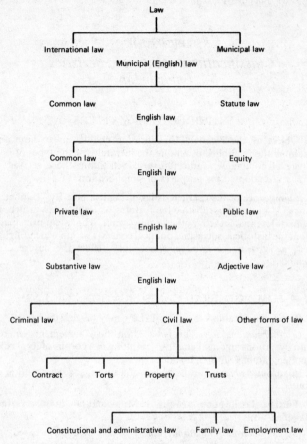

FIG.1 *Some classifications of law*.

the direct interest of the state and public in the results of proceedings, e.g. civil law, constitutional law.

(*d*) *Substantive law and adjective law*. This classification is based on:

(*i*) *substantive law*, which is concerned with the determination of rights, liabilities and duties, and which is administered by the courts;

(*ii*) *adjective law*, which is concerned with procedure and practice in the courts.

DETAILED CLASSIFICATION OF ENGLISH LAW

5. Essence of this classification. *See* Fig. 1. This classification takes into account the main divisions of English law as it is today. It recognises the separate nature of some of the branches, but emphasises common relationship and origin.

6. Classification. The following branches of law may be enumerated:

(*a*) *Criminal law*. This is concerned, essentially, with those offences which the state seeks to prevent, the commission of which may result in the imposition of penalties on offenders. It includes subsidiary classes, such as offences against the state, against persons, against property (*see* XII–XIV).

(*b*) *Civil law*. This is concerned with those branches of law relating to the rights and duties of individuals which arise out of their interrelationship as members of the community. It includes contract (the enforcing of legally binding agreements: *see* XV); torts (the infringement of legal rights not resulting exclusively from contract or trust and giving rise to actions for unliquidated damages: *see* XVI); land law (matters arising from the ownership, possession and transfer of real property: *see* XVII); trusts (matters arising from the relationship of trustee and beneficiary: *see* XVII).

(*c*) *Other branches*, e.g. constitutional and administrative law (*see* V, VI); family law (*see* XVIII); employment law (*see* XIX).

GENERAL CHARACTERISTICS OF ENGLISH LAW

7. Preliminary matters. The general characteristics of English law stem from its continuing growth and that, in turn, reflects the conditions of English life throughout the centuries. Changing moral and social standards have imprinted English law with attitudes rooted in an amalgam of religious thought, concepts of social responsibility, the needs of a developing industrial society, and, more recently, the idea of a welfare state.

8. Civil and common law countries. The legal system of the U.K. is characterised as a "common law" system, in contrast to that of, for example, France, where "civil law" dominates. The distinctive features of our common law system, which mark it off from a civil law system, include: the importance of precedent; the relatively minor role of authoritative texts in the interpretation of the law; the importance of the jury system; the use of accusatorial procedures.

9. Significance of the general characteristics of English law. The characteristics of our law reflect its growth; they account in part for the dominant role played in the formation of law by concepts of "justice" and "equality"; they reflect the dominance of the state as symbolised by Parliament's role in the legislative process.

FUNDAMENTAL CHARACTERISTICS OF ENGLISH LAW (1)

10. Preliminary matters: "fundamental" in what sense? By "fundamental" is meant general and basic, i.e. the characteristics which may be discerned by an examination of our law in practice.

11. Continuity. With the possible exception of the period of the Commonwealth (1649–60) our law has known no important breaches in continuity. There has been no "new beginning" as the result of a fundamental political upheaval, so that there is a clear line of development stretching back to the legal innovations of the Norman conquerors and, occasionally, beyond that era to Anglo-Saxon days.

12. Reflections of moral thought. Christian doctrine has often characterised the spirit of our laws. The courts today remain concerned with questions of morality: *see Shaw* v. *D.P.P.* (1961).

13. Reflections of social attitudes. Beliefs and attitudes relating to responsibility for the care of the weak and the needy, for example, have recently found expression in the growth of welfare law. *See*, for example, Social Security Acts 1979, 1980, 1981, 1983.

14. Pragmatism. Our law is based on no single legal theory. Its approach remains pragmatic, concerned with the practical side of matters, rather than any one ideology. Even the deep respect for the supremacy of common law has not invested it with any immutable characteristics or principles.

15. Not based on logic. Our law does not rest on any theory of logic, so that judicial decisions and statutes do not always obey the formal rules of logical systems. "The life of the law has not been logic; it has been experience": Holmes.

16. An amalgam: written and unwritten. English law has not been reduced in its entirety to written form; statute and custom co-exist as fundamentals of our law.

17. Not codified. English law remains uncodified. Some sections of the law have been reduced to codified form, e.g. Sale of Goods Act 1979. By and large, however, arguments for a single code (as it exists in some civil law countries) have not been accepted in this country.

FUNDAMENTAL CHARACTERISTICS OF ENGLISH LAW (2)

18. Only Parliament can make law. Legislation is now the prerogative of Parliament (*see* VI). This characteristic of English law is a reflection of the doctrine of Parliamentary supremacy, which reflects the significance of the will of the people—an essential feature of a legal system in a democratic state.

19. Only Parliament can lay down legal sanctions. This characteristic is allied with that mentioned in **18** above. Penalties for offences against the law are matters, initially, for Parliament alone.

20. Nullum crimen sine lege. "There is no crime except in accordance with the law." "The great leading rule of criminal law is that nothing is a crime unless it is plainly forbidden by law. This rule is no doubt subject to exceptions, but they are rare, narrow, and to be admitted with the greatest reluctance and only upon the strongest reasons": *per* Stephen L. J. in *R*. v. *Price* (1884).

21. All persons are equal before the law. English law does not generally recognise social status as a basis for favoured treatment in civil or criminal proceedings.

22. Presumption of innocence. A man is presumed innocent until his guilt is proved by the prosecution. "Throughout the web of English criminal law one golden thread is always to be seen, that it is the duty of the prosecution to prove the prisoner's guilt subject to ... the defence of insanity and subject also to any statutory exception.... No matter what the charge or where the trial, the principle that the prosecution must prove the guilt of the prisoner is part of the common law of England and no attempt to whittle it down can be entertained": *per* Viscount Sankey in *Woolmington* v. *D.P.P.* (1935).

23. Right of appeal. Under statute, a convicted person may have a general right of appeal to a higher court (*see* XI).

24. Importance of procedure. The importance of adjective law (*see* 4(*d*)(*ii*) above) is a vital characteristic of our law. The law of evidence (*see* X), its formalities and strict rules, exemplify the significance of procedure.

25. Justice in open court. With some few exceptions (e.g. cases relating to state security, some types of matrimonial proceedings) evidence is heard in open court and the judge gives his decision, and his reasons for that decision, in open court. It is "of fundamental importance that justice should not only be done, but should manifestly and undoubtedly be seen to be done": *per* Lord Hewart in *R.* v. *Sussex Justices, ex parte McCarthy* (1924).

26. Distinctive position of the English judiciary. Our judges are independent, in that they are not political appointees; their salaries are secured by Parliament; superior judges may not be dismissed save by resolution of Parliament; their statements in court are privileged so that their words may not be used as the basis of an action for defamation. The rare circumstances in which a judge may be dismissed are as follows:

(*a*) In the case of judges of the superior courts (except the Lord Chancellor, who holds his office at the sovereign's pleasure) they may be removed on an address by both Houses of Parliament, where they have failed to conduct themselves properly.

(*b*) In the case of circuit judges and recorders, they may be removed by the Lord Chancellor because of misbehaviour or incapacity, or, additionally in the case of recorders, because of failure to comply with the conditions of their appointment: *see* Courts Act 1971, ss. 17(4), 21(6). (*See* also a letter from J. R. Spencer in *The Times*, 12th December 1983, referring to the dismissal of judges in 1830, 1851 and 1983.)

(*c*) Magistrates may be removed by the Lord Chancellor without showing cause. Some have been removed for having refused to administer legislation with which they did not agree.

INQUISITORIAL AND ACCUSATORIAL PROCEDURES

27. Definitions. *Inquisitorial procedure* refers to a system under which the judge searches for facts, listens to witnesses, examines documents, and orders that evidence be taken, following which he may make further investigations. *Accusatorial procedure* refers to a system under which parties and their representatives have the primary responsibility for finding and presenting evidence, while the judge's role is that of umpire.

28. Importance of the distinction for English law. English law prefers, in general, the accusatorial form of procedure. This is seen clearly in the English law of evidence (*see* X) and in the part played by judge and counsel in civil and criminal proceedings.

PROGRESS TEST 3

1. State some of the general classifications of English law.   **(3, 4)**
2. What is meant by "adjective law"?   **(4)**

3. Enumerate some of the sections of law which make up "civil law". **(6)**

4. What is a "civil law country"? **(8)**

5. "English law is characterised by its continuity." Explain this statement. **(11)**

6. How does our law reflect morality and social attitudes? **(12, 13)**

7. Is our law based in any way on logic? **(15)**

8. How is Parliamentary supremacy reflected in some of the characteristics of English law? **(18, 19)**

9. Explain the phrase *nullum crimen sine lege*. **(20)**

10. What is the "presumption of innocence"? **(22)**

11. Explain the ways in which the independence of our judges is secured. **(26)**

12. What is the difference between the inquisitorial and the accusatorial procedures? **(27)**

CHAPTER IV

Some Basic Legal Concepts

INTRODUCTORY MATTERS

1. What is a "legal concept"? A "concept" may be described as an abstract idea. A "legal concept" is a theoretical notion concerning the attributes of certain expressions fundamental to our law.

2. Matters to be covered. The following important legal concepts touched upon below are:

    (*a*) rights and duties (*see* **4–10** below);
    (*b*) ownership and possession (*see* **11–14** below);
    (*c*) property (*see* **15–16** below);
    (*d*) legal personality (*see* **17–20** below).

3. The importance of terminology in legal concepts. The distinctive flavour of legal vocabulary is no more evident than in the paragraphs which follow. Everyday words such as "right", "ownership", "property", take on a precise, technical significance which must be kept in mind when these terms are discussed (*see* I, **3**).

RIGHTS AND DUTIES

4. Preliminary matters. Our law is concerned, in large measure, with the protection and enforcement of rights. A may have a *right* to walk over B's land; B prevents A from exercising that right, so that proceedings may be instituted for the recognition and enforcement of A's right. C has a *right* to enjoy the possession of his property; D disregards that right by dishonestly appropriating C's property, so that criminal proceedings are brought against D under the Theft Act 1968, arising from the disregarding of C's right. E has a *right* to enjoy his good reputation; F attempts to destroy that reputation by publishing libellous statements concerning E, so that, in subsequent proceedings for defamation, the assistance of the courts is sought to uphold E's right. The term "right" is used here in a narrow, but important, sense.

5. Definition of a legal right. A legal right is an interest which the law will recognise and protect, respect for which is a legal duty, disregard of which is a legal wrong. It should be noted that a right is of no consequence and, therefore, may be said to have no real existence, if it is not recognised *and* protected by the law. Further, a right of one person results in a *duty* adhering to another (*see* **8** below).

6. Characteristics of a legal right. Consider, as an example, the right to enjoy quiet (i.e. uninterrupted) possession of one's property:

(*a*) The right is *vested* in an owner; there are no rights not vested in persons.

(*b*) The right results in a duty on other persons who are thereby *bound*.

(*c*) The right results in an *obligation* upon some person to act, or not to act, in a way which favours the person owning that right.

(*d*) The right exists *in relation to* something.

7. Wrongs. The law must be concerned also with legal wrongs. Thus, it may be a moral wrong to covet one's neighbour's goods, or to entertain violent thoughts towards one's neighbour; neither of these mental activities constitutes a violation of the law. Often, however, that which is a moral wrong is also a legal wrong, e.g. stealing, murder. A legal wrong is an act or omission which is contrary to the rules of law and which may result from a disregard of the rights of others.

8. Duties. Rights involve duties. X's *right* may be Y's *duty*. Thus, if X has an exclusive right to graze his cattle on Y's land, Y has a duty to allow X's cattle to be brought on his land for that purpose. If A has a right to walk along the highway, B has a general duty not to prevent A's exercise of that right. "To ascribe a right to one person is to imply that some other person is under a corresponding duty": Salmond.

9. Definition of a legal duty. A legal duty is a legally recognised obligation to perform or abstain from performing some act.

10. Rights in personam and in rem. The law distinguishes the following rights:

(*a*) *Rights in personam.* These are rights of a personal nature available only against particular persons, e.g. X's right to receive rent from Y. Y alone has a duty to pay rent to X.

(*b*) *Rights in rem.* These are rights available against "the world at large", e.g. X's right to the occupation of his property. "The world at large" has the duty to respect X's right.

OWNERSHIP AND POSSESSION

11. Preliminary matters. Ownership and possession—concepts upon which much of our law of property rests—are not necessarily one and the same thing. X's car is stolen by Y. Y has possession of the car; its ownership remains vested in X. A leases a farm to B. B is in possession of the farm as lessee; X, as lessor, remains in ownership.

12. The concept of ownership. Ownership involves all those rights which arise between an owner and the subject-matter of that ownership. A's ownership of his farm includes, e.g. his right to enjoy possession of it, his right to lease or sell it and his right to use it for his own, lawful purposes. These and similar rights constitute, collectively, the quality of absolute ownership.

(*a*) *Vested ownership* refers to a perfect title of ownership, i.e. title (right) to the property residing absolutely in the owner, as where A buys goods from B and receives them after paying the agreed price. Ownership of the goods is vested in A.

(*b*) *Conditional ownership* refers to an imperfect title of ownership, i.e. conditional title to property, as where a testator leaves property to X if he should survive Y. In that case X has conditional ownership which will vest in him fully only upon Y's death.

13. Possession. Possession, described as "the most basic relationship between men and things", is based on some degree of physical control; it involves *corpus* (i.e. that which is possessed) and *animus possidendi* (i.e. intention to possess). It has been defined variously, e.g. as "physical detention coupled with an interest to use the thing detained as one's own" (Maine) and as "the continuing exercise of a claim to the exclusive use of some material object" (Salmond). *See Lockyer* v. *Gibb* (1967) (possession without mental element in relation to a crime). (Note that since ownership is based on a relationship *de jure*, i.e. rising out of a legal right, possession of the subject-matter is not generally necessary.)

14. Possession in fact and in law. Possession *in fact* is no more than the relationship between some person and some thing, based essentially on physical control. Possession *in law* arises where the possessor has legal rights in that which he possesses, i.e. he has title to it. The law will generally protect the latter, but not always the former (as where possession in fact arises out of violation of another's ownership).

PROPERTY

15. Preliminary matters. In law, property is essentially that which can be owned. Thus, a man can have no property in the air which we breathe. Property may be no more than an aggregate of rights; it may relate to various types of object. Thus, the Theft Act 1968, s. 4(1), refers to property as including "money and all other property, real or personal, including things in action and other intangible property".

16. Types of property. Property may be classified as follows:

(a) *Corporeal or incorporeal*, i.e. that which is material (a house) or that which is not material (a lease).

(b) *Movable and immovable*, i.e. that which may be transferred physically (a table) or that to which only title can be transferred (land).

(c) *Real and personal*, i.e. that which comprises rights over land (which were originally recoverable in a "real action") or that which is identical with movable property (which was originally recoverable in a "personal action").

LEGAL PERSONALITY

17. Preliminary matters. In general, a person is one considered by the law as capable of attracting rights or duties. The concept clearly applies to most human beings. But what of a corporation? Has a corporation rights or duties and can it be penalised, as can a human being, for violating rights or failing to perform duties? To solve these and similar problems, the law recognises a concept based on the recognition of human beings and legal, or "fictitious", persons.

18. Human beings and legal personality. Our law, in bestowing legal personality on human beings in general, considers that "persons are the substances of which rights and duties are the attributes". Human beings have rights and duties; they may also be deprived of those rights (as where a person has less than absolute rights over his property, or where he is imprisoned); they may be relieved of certain duties (as where a person is declared mentally unsound).

19. Legal persons and legal personality. Legal (or "fictitious" or "artificial") persons are creations of the law; personality has been attributed to them by the law. Examples are corporations, which may be considered as *corporations aggregate* (groups of co-existing persons, such as registered companies) or *corporations sole* (series of successive persons, e.g. the sovereign).

(a) A corporation is, in law, distinct from its members: *see Salomon* v. *Salomon* (1897).

(b) A corporation has rights and duties recognised by the law.

(c) A corporation may be held liable for legal wrongs: *see R.* v. *I.C.R. Haulage Co.* (1944); *Tesco* v. *Nattrass* (1972).

20. Legal status. This term is used to refer to a person's legal condition, his capacities and incapacities at law and his general position as recognised by the law.

PROGRESS TEST 4

1. What is meant by a "legal right"? **(5)**

2. What are the characteristics of a legal right? **(6)**

3. Is the law concerned with all types of wrong? **(7)**

4. Define a legal duty. **(9)**

5. What is the difference between rights *in personam* and rights *in rem*? **(10)**

6. Explain the concept of ownership. **(12)**

7. How is possession recognised? **(13)**

8. What type of possession exists in the relationship of a thief and the property he has stolen? **(14)**

9. Enumerate some of the classifications of property. **(16)**

10. Explain the concept of legal personality. **(17, 18)**

11. Does the law attribute legal personality to a limited company? **(19)**

12. What is meant by "legal status"? **(20)**

CHAPTER V

The British Constitution and the Rule of Law

INTRODUCTORY MATTERS

1. What is meant by a "constitution"? The term "constitution" is generally used in the following senses in law:

(*a*) To describe the *mode of organisation* of a state or society as embodied in those rules which are part of the law of the land or established by usage and convention. The expression "the British Constitution" is understood in this sense.

(*b*) To describe a *document* which embodies the principal rules of government, which becomes the authority for acts of government. The expression "the American Constitution" is generally understood in this sense.

2. Written and unwritten constitutions. The British Constitution is unwritten, never having been reduced to one document or a group of documents. It is to be comprehended by reference to statute, conventions, judicial decisions, etc. Some written constitutions, e.g. the Soviet Constitution, are embodied in documents which set out in precise form the fundamentals of government and legislation.

(*a*) Dicey wrote of a "flexible constitution" as "one under which every law of every description can be changed with the same ease and in the same manner by one and the same body", and a "rigid constitution" as "one under which certain laws generally known as constitutional or fundamental laws cannot be changed in the same manner as ordinary laws".

(*b*) The advantages of an unwritten constitution, such as the British Constitution, are said to be extreme flexibility, so that constitutional change can be made in order to reflect social change, and an absence of dogmatic constitutional law which can characterise a system dominated by a document "enshrining the law".

(*c*) The disadvantages of a written constitution are said to arise from the uncertainties produced where there is no ultimate "written" authority to which one can refer. (It should be noted that some legal writers are now calling for a Bill of Rights which would set out in unambiguous form the fundamental rights which we enjoy, but which have not been stated in a written, systematic form.)

3. Matters to be covered. The following topics are mentioned in this chapter:

    (a) the three institutions of government in Britain (*see* **4–7** below);

    (b) the separation of the powers (*see* **8–10** below);

    (c) the conventions of the Constitution (*see* **11–13** below);

    (d) the rule of law (*see* **14–16** below).

INSTITUTIONS OF GOVERNMENT

4. Preliminary matters. According to some writers, a constitution involves different types of legal powers—legislative, executive and judicial. The following fundamental institutions of government in Britain are noted below: the monarchy (*see* **5** below); the legislature (*see* **6** below); the executive (*see* **7** below).

5. The monarchy. The monarchy in Britain is a "constitutional", as opposed to an "absolute", monarchy. The Queen acts upon the advice of her ministers and, to that considerable extent, reigns but does not rule. Her power is hedged in by a variety of conventions.

    (a) The Queen symbolises the state. The business of government, carried on in her name, is performed by her ministers.

    (b) Succession to the throne is regulated by the Act of Settlement 1701.

    (c) Royal Assent to a Parliamentary Bill is essential (*see* VI, **13**).

    (d) Note the important constitutional maxim: "The Queen can do no wrong". (The Crown Proceedings Act 1947, however, allows the Crown to be subject to most liabilities in tort.)

6. The legislature. The legislature is a trinity comprising the Queen, the Lords and the Commons (*see* VI, **1**). It is invested with power—as is no other body in the country—to make, alter and repeal laws.

7. The executive. The executive is usually considered as comprising the following institutions:

    (a) *The Privy Council*. This body, headed by a minister (Lord President of the Council) gives formal legal sanction to the government's executive orders.

    (b) *The Ministry*. This is, in fact, the government, headed by the Prime Minister. He or she forms a Cabinet, comprising principal ministers, and a ministry which includes the Cabinet and other ministers who head government departments.

    (c) *Government departments*. These are the real executive instruments of government. Staffed by civil servants, they advise on policy and execute government policies. Examples are the Treasury, Ministry of Defence and Department of Education and Science.

(*d*) *Government agencies*. These are bodies responsible for the day-to-day running of state-owned industries and other institutions. Examples are the National Coal Board and the Atomic Energy Authority.

THE SEPARATION OF POWERS

8. Preliminary matters. "The legislature should make, the executive should execute, and the judiciary should construe, the law." This division of power, approved by many legal writers, does not exist in practice in this country. Differences between the law-making functions of Parliament and the law-making which effectively ensues from the recognition of judicial precedent tend to be blurred. (Note, for example, the functions of the Lord Chancellor, mentioned in VII, **31**.) *See Duport Steels* v. *Sirs* (1980).

9. The theory of separation of powers. This owes its development to the French writer, Montesquieu, who elaborated in *The Spirit of the Laws* (1748) his belief (based on a faulty understanding of the British system of government) that "constant experience shows us that every man invested with power is apt to abuse it, and to carry his authority as far as it will go". Consequently, a government will be safe only if the three powers (legislature, executive and judiciary) are totally separated, i.e. independent of one another and distributed among different groups of persons able to hold one another in check. (Thus, the judge ought not to be a Member of Parliament; the civil servant ought not to be a judge.)

10. The theory today. It is not always easy to determine with precision the exact functions of the institutions of government. Jennings states, with reference to the separation of powers in the U.K., that the real safeguard against tyranny rests not in a precise delineation of institutional functions, "but in democratic control through an elected House of Commons in which the party system makes criticism open and effective".

CONVENTIONS OF THE CONSTITUTION

11. Parliamentary matters. Our constitution, unwritten and based in part on conventions tacitly agreed and resulting from long practice, can be seen as relying for its efficient working on many practices based on no legal rules. Thus, there is no law stating that Parliament must be convoked at least once a year; in practice this is invariably done.

12. Definition of constitutional conventions. Dicey defined these as "rules for determining the mode in which the discretionary powers of the Crown (or of ministers as servants of the Crown) ought to be exercised".

13. Examples of conventions. The acceptance of constitutional conventions, which do not rest on legal rules, may be seen in the following practices:

(*a*) A Ministry which has lost the confidence of the House of Commons must, generally, resign.

(*b*) The party with a majority in the Commons is entitled to have its leader made Prime Minister.

(*c*) A Cabinet is responsible collectively to Parliament for the general conduct of the executive.

(*d*) Lay peers do not participate in judicial proceedings in the House of Lords.

(*e*) The monarch must assent to a bill passed by both Houses.

THE RULE OF LAW

14. Preliminary matters. The phrase "rule of law" is used in several distinctive senses:

(*a*) *A legal maxim*, e.g. it is a "rule of law" that a child under the age of ten cannot form a guilty intention (*see* now Children and Young Persons Act 1933, s. 50, and Children and Young Persons Act 1963, s. 16).

(*b*) *Respect for the traditions and decisions of the courts*, e.g. it is said that civilisation cannot flourish in a society in which the "rule of law" is not respected.

(*c*) *The concept derived from the writings of Dicey* (*see* **16** below), that, ultimately, governmental powers must rest on law.

15. Rule of law and freedom. *See* **14**(*b*) above. In I, **6**, the case was argued for the dependence of freedom on law. Acceptance of the rule of law in a community is a prerequisite of freedom; where that acceptance is significantly qualified or rejected, there is a danger of the withering away of the force of law and of the freedom which rests on it. Where, for example, there is large-scale refusal to accept the full implications of the courts' decisions, or where important laws are ignored consistently by large numbers of people, the law has fallen into disrepute. Often, this precedes a general collapse of the legal and political order. Hence the importance, in our society, of an understanding of the basis of the rule of law and the freedoms which flow from it.

16. The rule of law: Dicey's concept. In *Law of the Constitution* (1885) Dicey argued that the "rule of law" denoted three vital principles:

(*a*) The regular law of the land takes precedence over the arbitrary exercise of government and discretionary powers.

(*b*) There must be no special privileges for officials. Equality before the law for citizens and officials demands that both be subject to the jurisdiction of the ordinary courts.

(*c*) The fundamental rights enjoyed by a citizen should arise from the ordinary law, not from any special guarantee by a constitution.

There are many today who call emphatically for a continuing appraisal of the actions of the executive, in its exercise of discretionary powers of rule-making, in the light of Dicey's principles.

PROGRESS TEST 5

1. What are the advantages of an unwritten constitution? **(2)**
2. Enumerate the institutions of government in the U.K. **(4)**
3. What are the functions of the monarchy in government? **(5)**
4. What is the "executive"? **(7)**
5. Explain the theory of separation of powers. **(8, 9)**
6. What is a constitutional convention? **(12)**
7. Give examples of conventions from Parliamentary procedure. **(13)**
8. Comment on Dicey's concept of the "rule of law". **(16)**

CHAPTER VI

Parliament at Work: the Process of Legislation

INTRODUCTORY MATTERS

1. The Queen in Parliament. Legislation in the U.K. results from the exercise of power by "the Queen in Parliament", i.e. the sovereign, House of Lords and House of Commons.

(*a*) *The House of Lords*, the upper House of Parliament, is composed of the Lords Spiritual (archbishops and bishops) and the Lords Temporal (hereditary and life peers).

(*b*) *The House of Commons*, the lower House of Parliament, consists of 650 members who are elected by popular franchise, each of whom represents a constituency in the U.K.

2. Public and private Acts. Acts of Parliament (i.e. statutes) may be public or private.

(*a*) *A public Act* relates to matters of public policy and generally applies to the U.K. as a whole.

(*b*) *A private Act* relates, generally, to the conferring of powers or benefits on persons or bodies of persons, e.g. local authorities, corporations.

3. Matters to be discussed. The following aspects of legislation are touched upon below:

(*a*) stages in the progress of a Bill through Parliament (*see* **4–13** below);

(*b*) citation and format of an Act (*see* **14–15** below);

(*c*) interpretation of statutes (*see* **16–20** below);

(*d*) delegated legislation (*see* **21–24** below).

PASSAGE OF A BILL THROUGH PARLIAMENT

4. Preliminary matters. A bill is no more than a draft statute. It becomes law (i.e. as an Act of Parliament) only when it has received the approval of Parliament. This approval necessitates a complex, often lengthy, procedure involving both Houses and, finally, the Royal Assent.

5. Stages in procedure. The following are the stages in the procedure necessary for the passage of a public Bill through Parliament:

  (a) introduction of the Bill (*see* **6** below);
  (b) First Reading (*see* **7** below);
  (c) Second Reading (*see* **8** below);
  (d) Committee stage (*see* **9** below);
  (e) Report stage (*see* **10** below);
  (f) Third Reading (*see* **11** below);
  (g) consideration of amendments (*see* **12** below);
  (h) Royal Assent (*see* **13** below).

6. Introduction of the Bill. Bills may be introduced in the Commons or Lords. For the purpose of this chapter, it is assumed that a public Bill is being introduced into the House of Commons. (There is a slightly different procedure in the case of a private Bill.) It may be introduced in one of three ways:

  (a) upon an order of the House;
  (b) upon presentation by a minister or private member after notice has been given (the usual method); or
  (c) upon its being brought down from the Lords, after a member of the Commons has shown an intention of taking charge of it.

7. First Reading. This is a formality, consisting of the Clerk of the House reading its short title. There is no debate and the Bill is ordered to be printed.

8. Second Reading. This is probably the most important stage in the Bill's passage through Parliament. It is considered and, following debate, a vote is taken. If the Bill passes its second reading it is progressed to the next step.

9. Committee stage. The Bill is next considered in great detail, clause by clause, often word by word, by a Standing Committee or a Committee of the whole House. Amendments are moved and voted upon. The formal rules of debate are relaxed, allowing members to speak on more than one occasion, so that this stage is often lengthy.

10. Report stage. The amended Bill is considered next by the House of Commons. It may be committed once more to a Select or Standing Committee.

11. Third Reading. There is rarely debate at this stage and the Bill is accepted or rejected. It then goes to the House of Lords, where it passes through the stages indicated above.

12. Consideration of amendments. The Lords' amendments to the Bill are discussed. Where there is disagreement between the Houses a compromise is usually reached by one House conceding the objections it has raised.

13. Royal Assent. The Royal Assent, which must be given, transforms the Bill into an Act of Parliament. (The Royal Assent was last refused by Queen Anne in 1707.)

NOTE: Under the Parliament Acts 1911 and 1949 a money Bill (i.e. a Bill creating a charge upon the public revenues, or altering taxation) may be presented for Royal Assent without the consent of the Lords if it has been passed by the Commons and referred to the Lords at least one month before the end of a Parliamentary session and it has not been passed by the Lords without amendment within one month following the date on which it was sent to them.

CITATION AND FORMAT OF AN ACT

14. Method of citation. Citation means the method of referring to an Act by its title. The citation title of an Act usually appears in the final clause and is usually identical with the short title which heads the Act (*see* **15** below). *See*, for example, National Heritage Act 1983, s. 43: "This Act may be cited as the National Heritage Act 1983."

(*a*) In early days, statutes were cited by the name of the place at which Parliament met, e.g. "Provisions of Oxford 1258".

(*b*) Later, they were cited by reference to regnal year and chapter. Thus, the Perjury Act 1911 was cited as "1 & 2 Geo. V, c.6", i.e. the sixth of the statutes passed in the Parliamentary session which extended over the first and second years of the reign of George V.

(*c*) The Act of Parliament Numbering and Citation Act 1962 abolished the mode of citation referred to at (*b*) above. An Act passed after 1st January 1963 is now cited by referring to its short title, calendar year and chapter number, e.g. Trade Descriptions Act 1968 (c. 29).

15. Format of an Act. Reference should be made to the facsimile Act on pp. 38–39. Note the following points:

(*a*) *Short title*. It is by this that the Act is generally known.

(*b*) *Number*. This indicates that the Act is the eighth to have received the Royal Assent in 1977.

(*c*) *Long title*. This describes the purpose of the legislation embodied in the Act.

(*d*) *Date of Act*. This is the date on which the Act received Royal Assent, thus becoming law.

(*e*) *Enacting words*. This formal statement records the responsibility for legislation of the Queen in Parliament, i.e. Her Majesty, Lords and Commons.

(*f*) *Sections and subsections*. Acts are generally divided and subdivided in this manner, so that references may be abbreviated thus: Job Release Act 1977, s. 1(2).

(*g*) *Marginal notes*. These may be explanatory of the Act's clauses. In general, they are not considered to form part of the Act, but they must be examined by the court in the case of an ambiguity.

(*h*) *Interpretation*. This type of clause explains some terms and phrases used in the Act.

(*i*) *Citation*. The title by which the Act may be cited is usually that at the head, i.e. the short title.

(*j*) *Extent of operation*. These words refer to the geographical area in which the Act will operate.

INTERPRETATION OF STATUTES

16. Preliminary matters. It is one thing for Parliament to agree to the wording of an Act, but quite another for the courts to interpret the words of which the Act consists. The words of a statute may be ambiguous (*see Fisher* v. *Bell* (1961)) or uncertain (*see Griffin* v. *Squires* (1958)). *Per* Lord Denning in *Seaford Court Estates Ltd.* v. *Asher* (1949): "It must be remembered that it is not within human powers to foresee the manifold set of facts which may arise, and, even if it were, it is not possible to provide for them in terms free from all ambiguity."

17. General approach to interpretation. There are three important approaches to the ascertainment of Parliament's intentions as expressed in an Act which may be used by the court in the task of interpretation:

(*a*) *The "literal rule"*. Parliament's intention must be found in the ordinary, natural and literal meaning of the words of the statute. Note, however, the comment of Lord Denning in *Corocraft* v. *Pan American Airways* (1969): "... the literal meaning of the words is never allowed to prevail where it would produce manifest absurdity or consequences which can never have been intended by the legislature".

c. 8   1

ELIZABETH II

Job Release Act 1977 ◄──────── Short title

1977 CHAPTER 8 ◄──────── Number

An Act to provide finance for job release schemes; and ◄──── Long title
for a connected purpose.   [30th March 1977] ◄──── Date of Act

B E IT ENACTED by the Queen's most Excellent Majesty, by and
with the advice and consent of the Lords Spiritual and
Temporal, and Commons, in this present Parliament ◄──── Enacting words
assembled, and by the authority of the same, as follows:—

Section ──► **1.**—(1) There shall be paid out of voted money any sums Financial
required by the Secretary of State or the Department of Manpower authorisation, ◄── Marginal note
Services for Northern Ireland in paying during a period for etc.
which this section has effect temporary allowances to persons
approaching pensionable age, under schemes made and imple-
mented with a view to creating job vacancies and otherwise
mitigating the effects of high unemployment.

Subsection ──► (2) The scale of the allowances, the circumstances in which
they are to be paid and the conditions of payment shall be such
as the Treasury or, as the case may be, the Department of Finance
for Northern Ireland may approve from time to time.

(3) As subsection (1) operates as authority for the payment of
allowances during a period it also operates as authority for
payment of an allowance after the expiration of the period to a
person whose application for an allowance has been approved
in the period.

(4) This section has effect—

(a) for the period of eighteen months beginning with the
passing of this Act, and

(b) *The "golden rule".* The words of a statute should be interpreted
according to their ordinary grammatical meaning as far as that is
possible, but only to the extent that the result is not manifestly
absurd. "It is a very useful rule in the construction of a statute to
adhere to the ordinary meaning of the words used, and to the grammatical construction, unless that is at variance with the intention of
the legislature to be collected from the statute itself, or leads to any
manifest absurdity or repugnance, in which case the language may
be varied or modified so as to avoid such inconvenience, but no
further": *per* Parke B. in *Becke* v. *Smith* (1836). *See also Federal
Steam Navigation Co.* v. *Department of Trade* (1974); *Sanders* v.
Richmond L.B.C. (1978)—interpretation of "arrangements" in Sex

(*b*) for such subsequent periods as the Secretary of State may by order made by statutory instrument provide for it to have effect,

but no one order shall provide for this section to have effect for more than twelve months.

(5) An order under this section shall not be made unless a draft of it has been laid before the House of Commons and approved by a resolution of that House.

(6) In subsection (1)—

(*a*) " voted money " means money provided by Parliament ◄──── Interpretation or, in Northern Ireland, money appropriated for the purposes of this Act; and

(*b*) " pensionable age " has the same meaning as in the legislation relating to social security.

(7) Provisions enabling a person to qualify for the allowance by reference to the time within which he or she will attain pensionable age are not, nor ever were, discriminatory for any purpose of the law relating to sex discrimination.

Citation and extent.   **2.**—(1) This Act may be cited as the Job Release Act 1977. ◄──── Citation

(2) This Act extends to Northern Ireland. ◄──── Extent of operation

PRINTED IN ENGLAND BY BERNARD M. THIMONT
Controller of Her Majesty's Stationery Office and Queen's Printer of Acts of Parliament

LONDON: PUBLISHED BY HER MAJESTY'S STATIONERY OFFICE
10p net
ISBN 0 10 540877 8

(384240)

Discrimination Act 1975, s. 6(1); *Tower Hamlets L.B.C.* v. *Creitzman* (1984)—covered market held to be a "square" and therefore properly within the definition of "street' contained in Control of Pollution Act 1974, s. 62(1); *Hammond* v. *N.C.B.* (1984)—interpretation of "working place" for the purposes of Mines and Quaries Act 1954, s. 48; *Lanham* v. *Rickwood* (1984)—meaning of "drunk" in relation to Criminal Justice Act 1967, s. 91.

(*c*) *The "mischief rule"*. This was defined in *Heydon's Case* (1584): "Four things are to be discussed and considered: (1) what was the common law before the making of the Act; (2) what was the mischief and defect for which the common law did not provide; (3) what remedy Parliament hath resolved and appointed to cure the disease of the commonwealth; and (4) the true reason of the remedy." *See also Maunsell* v. *Olins* (1975).

18. Further rules. The following further rules of interpretation of statutes should be noted:

(*a*) The statute is to be read as a whole: *see Beswick* v. *Beswick* (1968).

(*b*) General words which follow two or more particular words in a statute are to be confined to a meaning of the same kind as those particular words (the *ejusdem generis* rule): *see Customs and Excise Commissioners* v. *Savoy Hotel* (1966). Thus, in *Gregory* v. *Fearn* (1953) that part of the Sunday Observance Act 1677 which reads "... no tradesman, artificer, workman, labourer *or other person whatsoever*", was held *not* to have reference to an estate agent.

(*c*) A penal provision of a statute is to be construed narrowly, and generally in favour of the individual: *see R.* v. *Hallam* (1957).

19. Presumptions in statutory interpretation. The following presumptions (*see* X, **17**) should be noted:

(*a*) A statute is not to be taken as effecting a fundamental alteration in the general law unless it uses words pointing unmistakably to that conclusion: *see National Assistance Board* v. *Wilkinson* (1952).

(*b*) There is a presumption against the statutory imposition of liability without fault: *see Sweet* v. *Parsley* (1970).

(*c*) There is a presumption against depriving a person of a right invested in him: *see Metropolitan Asylum District* v. *Hill* (1881); *Allen* v. *Gulf Oil Refining Ltd.* (1981).

(*d*) There is a presumption that a statute does not bind the Crown: *see BBC* v. *Johns* (1965).

(*e*) There is a presumption against the ousting of the court's jurisdiction: *see Pyx Granite Ltd.* v. *Ministry of Housing* (1960).

20. Intrinsic and extrinsic aids to interpretation. Aids to the interpretation of statutes may be intrinsic or extrinsic.

(*a*) *Intrinsic aids* are found within the statute itself, e.g. its titles (long and short), its preamble (which precedes the enacting words and states the "reason" for the statute), the headings and the interpretation section. *See D.P.P.* v. *Schildkamp* (1971).

(*b*) *Extrinsic, or external, aids* include dictionaries (*see* Ripon Housing Order 1938 (1939)) and other statutes containing similar words (*see R.* v. *Herrod* (1976)). *See* also *Hadmor Productions* v. *Hamilton* (1982).

DELEGATED LEGISLATION

21. Preliminary matters. Because of the complicated nature of administration in the U.K., Parliament delegates specific powers to other bodies, empowering them, in limited circumstances, to create bye-laws, rules, orders, etc. Such delegated legislation must be within the powers conferred by Parliament, otherwise it is invalid. Types of delegated legislation considered below are:

(*a*) Orders in Council (*see* **22** below);
(*b*) statutory instruments (*see* **23** below);
(*c*) bye-laws (*see* **24** below).

22. Orders in Council. These are decrees of the sovereign issued with the advice of the Privy Council. They may be used, for example, to bring an Act into operation.

23. Statutory instruments. These are rules and regulations made by ministers and government departments under authority of statute: *see* Statutory Instruments Act 1946. They are cited by name, year and number, e.g. Air Navigation (Noise Certification) Order 1984 (S.I. 1984 No. 368).

24. Bye-laws. Bye-laws are made by local authorities under powers conferred by statute. They take effect only within the area of the authority which makes them: *see* Local Government Act 1972. Bye-laws are examined by a confirming authority, e.g. a government department which is empowered to accept or reject them.

NOTE: "Autonom legislation" refers to the rights of an autonomous body, e.g. the Law Society, to legislate for its own members.

PROGRESS TEST 6

1. What is meant by the "Queen in Parliament"? **(1)**
2. Explain the difference between a public and a private Act. **(2)**
3. Enumerate the stages in the passage of a public Bill through Parliament. **(5)**
4. Explain "First" and "Second" Readings of a Bill. **(7, 8)**
5. Comment on the method of citation of a statute. **(14)**
6. Why is the interpretation of statutes a matter of importance in law? **(16)**
7. Explain the "golden rule" used in statutory interpretation. **(17)**

8. Outline some of the presumptions in statutory interpretation. **(19)**

9. Comment on the use of intrinsic aids in statutory interpretation. **(20)**

10. What are statutory instruments?   **(23)**

CHAPTER VII

The Courts and the Personnel of the Law

INTRODUCTORY MATTERS

1. Nature of the courts. The ancient theory of the sovereign as "the fountain of justice" finds a reflection in the work of the courts which, in a sense, dispense justice "in the name of the Queen". The functions of the Queen in Parliament (*see* VI, **1**) are also reflected, not only in the law which is dispensed by the courts, but, also, in the legal basis of the courts' structure: *see*, for example, Supreme Court Act 1981 (referred to in this chapter as "S.C.A. 1981"). The term "court" is used in English law to indicate the place where judicial proceedings take place *and* to refer to the judge or judges who constitute the court.

2. Classification of courts. Courts may be classified generally in the following manner:

(*a*) *Superior and inferior courts.* Superior courts are those which are not subject in any way, save in matters of appeal, to any other court, e.g. High Court of Justice, Court of Appeal. Inferior courts are those subject to other courts, e.g. county courts. (The term "supreme courts" is also applied to those whose decisions are final, e.g. House of Lords.)

(*b*) *Civil and criminal.* This classification is based on the general nature of the work carried out by the courts. It should be noted, however, that some courts, e.g. magistrates' courts and the Crown Court, have both civil and criminal jurisdiction.

(*c*) *Original and appellate.* Courts of original jurisdiction, e.g. the magistrates' courts, known also as courts of first instance, are distinguished from those which hear appeals, e.g. Court of Appeal, House of Lords. It should be noted, however, that some courts, e.g. the Crown Court, may exercise both an original *and* an appellate jurisdiction.

(*d*) *Courts of record and courts which are not courts of record.* This is an ancient classification based on whether or not a court kept a record of its proceedings and decisions and whether or not it could punish for contempt. Under this classification, courts-martial, which are not empowered to punish for contempt, were differentiated from, e.g. the Crown Court, which can punish for contempt.

THE CIVIL COURTS

3. The county courts. These courts were established under the County Courts Act 1846 to provide a system of courts to deal with small claims. They cover over 300 districts, each with its own county court, grouped into circuits, to each of which a circuit judge is assigned. *See* now County Courts Act 1984.

(*a*) *Jurisdiction.* Under the County Courts Act 1984 jurisdiction relates to matters concerning:

(*i*) actions founded on contract or tort (excluding libel and slander) not exceeding an amount fixed by the Lord Chancellor;

(*ii*) actions relating to land of a rateable value not exceeding an amount fixed by the Lord Chancellor;

(*iii*) matters relating to equity, e.g. trusts, partnerships, mortgages, not exceeding an amount fixed by the Lord Chancellor;

(*iv*) winding-up of companies where the paid-up capital is less than an amount fixed by the Lord Chancellor;

(*v*) some functions relating to guardianship, and adoption. About 150 statutes give the county court additional jurisdiction. For details, *see* the current "Green Book", *County Court Practice*.

(*b*) *Composition.* The county court is staffed by nominated circuit judges and registra. A judge sits, generally without a jury, save where, for example, fraud is being considered, when a jury of eight may be called. A registrar acts in the capacity of an assistant judge.

4. The High Court of Justice. The High Court was created by the Judicature Acts 1873–75 and consisted of five divisions: Queen's Bench; Chancery; Probate, Divorce and Admiralty; Exchequer; and Crown Pleas (the last two being merged in the Queen's Bench Division in 1880). Under the Administration of Justice Act 1970, the Probate, Divorce and Admiralty Division was renamed the Family Division, and Admiralty work was transferred to the Queen's Bench Division to be exercised by a separate Admiralty Court. The High Court of Justice consists today of the Queen's Bench Division, Chancery Division (including the Patents Court set up under the Patents Act 1977) and the Family Division. *See* S.C.A. 1981, s. 5.

(*a*) *Jurisdiction.* This extends over England and Wales, but not to Scotland, the Isle of Man, the Channel Islands or beyond territorial waters. Sittings may take place anywhere in England or Wales. In general, all jurisdiction vested in the High Court belongs to all the divisions alike (*see* S.C.A. 1981, s. 5(5)).

(*b*) *Composition.* There are seventy-five High Court judges (known as puisne judges) (*see* **38** below).

5. Queen's Bench Division. This great common law court has a very important role in our legal system. (*See also* **22** below.) *See* S.C.A. 1981, s. 5.

(*a*) *Jurisdiction*. Its jurisdiction is civil and criminal, original and appellate. In its civil role it is concerned with actions in contract and tort. Jurisdiction over commercial matters may be exercised by the Commercial Court, Admiralty jurisdiction by the Admiralty Court. Three of its judges also hear cases in the Restrictive Practices Court, and one is appointed to hear cases before the Employment Appeal Tribunal.

(*b*) *Composition*. There are forty-five puisne judges in the Queen's Bench Division, in addition to the Lord Chief Justice.

6. Queen's Bench Divisional Court. This appeal court exercises the appellate jurisdiction of the Queen's Bench Division. *See* S.C.A. 1981, s. 5 and Sch. 1.

(*a*) *Jurisdiction*. This extends (in civil cases) to supervisory matters relating to inferior courts and tribunals by way of applications for prerogative writs (*mandamus, certiorari* and *prohibition*) and writs of *habeas corpus* (commanding a person who is detaining another in custody to "produce the body" of that person before the court). It may also hear appeals from the Solicitors' Disciplinary Tribunal, matters relating to disputed Parliamentary elections, and criminal appeals on points of law by way of case stated directly from a magistrates' court (or through the Crown Court).

(*b*) *Composition*. The appeal court consists of two to three judges, who may include the Lord Chief Justice. *See* S.C.A. 1981, s. 66 (1), (3).

7. Chancery Division. This Division is concerned generally with matters which were dealt with by the Court of Chancery before the Judicature Acts 1873–75. *See* the S.C.A. 1981, s. 5 and Sch. 1.

(*a*) *Jurisdiction*. This embraces partnership actions, execution of trusts, company law matters, revenue matters, conveyancing and land law matters, mortgages, administration of estates, rectification of deeds, and contentious probate cases.

(*b*) *Composition*. Ten Chancery judges are presided over by the Lord Chancellor and a Vice-Chancellor.

8. Chancery Divisional Court. This appeal court exercises the appellate jurisdiction of the Chancery Division.

(*a*) *Jurisdiction*. The court hears income tax appeals from the Commissioners of Inland Revenue and appeals from county courts relating to bankruptcy, etc. *See* Taxes Management Act 1970, s. 56.

(b) *Composition.* A single judge hears income tax appeals; otherwise at least two judges of the division sit to hear appeals.

9. Family Division. This division was created in 1970. *See* now S.C.A. 1981, s. 61(1) and Sch. 1.

(a) *Jurisdiction.* The division has an exclusive jurisdiction over most matrimonial disputes, grant of legal title to executors and matters relating to legitimacy, guardianship, adoption, etc.

(b) *Composition.* A President heads the division and is assisted by sixteen High Court judges.

10. Family Divisional Court. This appeal court exercises the appellate jurisdiction of the Family Division.

(a) *Jurisdiction.* It hears appeals from decisions of magistrates' courts, county courts and the Crown Court in matters concerning family law, affiliation, maintenance and adoption orders.

(b) *Composition.* Two judges hear appeals.

11. Court of Appeal (Civil Division). Since the Criminal Appeal Act 1966, the Court of Appeal has consisted of a civil and a criminal division. Appeal to the Civil Division generally lies as of right, but leave is required in certain cases, e.g. from determination of an appeal by a divisional court of the High Court; from an interlocutory order made by a judge; from the decision of a county court judge where the claim is small. *See* S.C.A. 1981, ss. 15–18.

(a) *Jurisdiction.* Appeals are heard from the High Court, county courts, the Employment Appeal Tribunal and the Restrictive Practices Court.

(b) *Composition.* The court consists of the Lord Chancellor, Lord Chief Justice, Master of the Rolls, President of the Family Division, former Lord Chancellors, Lords of Appeal in Ordinary and Lords Justices of Appeal. In practice, however, only the Master of the Rolls and Lords Justices of Appeal sit. Three judges usually form a court, but in a case of unusual importance a "full court" of five judges may be constituted. *See* S.C.A. 1981, s. 2.

12. House of Lords. The House of Lords is the final court of appeal in civil matters. (*See* also **24** below.)

(a) *Jurisdiction.* Appeals are heard from the Court of Appeal with leave of that court or the Appeals Committee of the House. (For the "leapfrog procedure" *see* XI, **6**.)

(b) *Composition.* The work of the House of Lords in its judicial role is performed by Lords of Appeal in Ordinary (the Law Lords), the Lord Chancellor, ex-Lord Chancellors, Master of the Rolls and peers who have held high judicial office. Lay peers do not participate in the hearing of appeals. The quorum is three, but, generally, five judges hear appeals. *See* Appellate Jurisdiction Act 1876.

13. Judicial Committee of the Privy Council. This was created by the Judicial Committee Act 1833. Its decisions, which do not bind English courts, carry, nevertheless, a considerable weight of authority. (*See* also **25** below.)

(*a*) *Jurisdiction.* This is derived from the Sovereign in Council. The Judicial Committee of the Privy Council does not "deliver judgment"; it "tenders advice" to the sovereign. It hears appeals from courts outside the U.K., e.g. the Isle of Man, the Channel Islands, Commonwealth countries, and appeals from ecclesiastical courts and medical tribunals. *See*, e.g., *Thomas* v. *The Queen* (1980); *Badry* v. *D.P.P. of Mauritius* (1982).

(*b*) *Composition.* The Judicial Committee of the Privy Council comprises the Lord President of the Council, Lord Chancellor, Lords of Appeal in Ordinary and members of the Privy Council who hold, or have held, high judicial office. In practice, however, only the Lord Chancellor and three to five Lords of Appeal in Ordinary sit.

14. Ecclesiastical courts. These courts exercise a measure of control over the clergy of the Church of England.

(*a*) *Jurisdiction.* Matters relating to doctrine and ritual of the church are within the consistory courts' jurisdiction.

(*b*) *Composition.* A consistory court is made up of a chancellor (appointed by a bishop). Appeal lies eventually to a Commission of Review composed of three Lords of Appeal in Ordinary and two Lords Spiritual (*see* VI, **1**(*a*)).

15. Restrictive Practices Court. This court was created under the Restrictive Trade Practices Act 1956. (*See* now Restrictive Trade Practices Act 1976.)

(*a*) *Jurisdiction.* It considers cases referred to it by the Director General of Fair Trading, or by parties to a restrictive agreement who have been ordered to give particulars to the court. It declares, for example, whether particular restrictions are or are not contrary to the public interest. Appeal lies to the Court of Appeal.

(*b*) *Composition.* The court is presided over by a High Court judge and includes other High Court judges, a judge of the Court of Session of Scotland, and of the Supreme Court of Northern Ireland, and up to ten lay members. *See* 1976 Act, s. 1(2).

16. Court of Protection. This court administers property and affairs of persons incapable, by reason of mental disorder, of managing their own affairs. *See* Mental Health Act 1983, Part VII.

(a) *Jurisdiction*. "... Exclusive jurisdiction over all the property and all the affairs of the patient in all their aspects; but not the management or care of the patient's person": *per* Ungoed-Thomas J., in *Re W.* (1971).

(b) *Composition*. Judges of the Supreme Court, nominated by the Lord Chancellor. (*See* Mental Health Act 1983, s. 93.)

17. Coroners' courts. Coroners' courts, which date from the twelfth century, are concerned with matters such as "treasure trove", but, principally, with inquests.

(a) *Jurisdiction*. This relates largely to deaths of persons dying within the coroner's district where there is reasonable cause for suspecting a violent or otherwise unnatural death, or a sudden death from causes unknown. An inquest may necessitate a jury of seven to eleven, whose verdict is recorded in an "inquisition". *See* Coroners Acts 1887–1980; Criminal Law Act 1977, s. 56 and Sch. 10; Administration of Justice Act 1982, s. 62; Coroners' Juries Act 1983; Coroners Rules 1984 (S.I. 1984 No. 552).

(b) *Composition*. The coroner (*see* **30** below), together with a jury where necessary. A divisional court can review a coroner's inquest (*see R.* v. *Greater Manchester Coroner* (1984)).

18. Employment Appeal Tribunal. This body was set up under the Employment Protection Act 1975. Appeal is to the Court of Appeal.

(a) *Jurisdiction*. The tribunal hears appeals on questions of law relating to decisions of tribunals on, for example, redundancy matters and allegations of discriminatory acts. It may hear applications for compensation from persons unreasonably excluded from unions. (*See* Employment Act 1980, ss. 4, 5.)

(b) *Composition*. The tribunal consists of judges of the High Court, Court of Appeal, Court of Session and lay members.

19. European Court of Justice. The court is, in effect, the supreme court of the European Communities: *see* Treaty of Rome 1957, art. 177. *See also* II, **28–30**.

(a) *Jurisdiction*. The court is concerned with the interpretation of the Treaty and with disputes arising from the application of its provisions. It sits in Luxembourg and expresses its opinions on judgments.

(b) *Composition*. The court consists of up to twelve judges, assisted by up to six advocates-general, who are not members of the court, but who advise by making reasoned submissions to the court.

THE CRIMINAL COURTS

20. Magistrates' courts. These courts (some 700 today) have a jurisdiction which is civil and criminal. (The civil jurisdiction includes, for example, recovery of some civil debts, renewal of licences, adoption orders and matrimonial orders.) The courts' criminal jurisdiction is extensive: *see* Magistrates' Courts Act 1980; Justices of the Peace Act 1979.

(*a*) *Jurisdiction.* This relates to offences which are classified as summary, indictable, or triable either way (*see* XII, **4**(*b*)).

(*b*) *Composition.* A court must consist of two to seven justices of the peace. A single lay magistrate may conduct a preliminary investigation. A stipendiary magistrate (appointed in the larger cities: *see* **29** below) has all the legal powers of two lay justices.

21. The Crown Court. The court was created by the Courts Act 1971 and sits regularly at ninety centres. (In London it is known as the Central Criminal Court—the "Old Bailey".) *See* S.C.A. 1981, ss. 73–87.

(*a*) *Jurisdiction.* The court is concerned with trials on indictment for offences wherever committed. It may also hear appeals from persons convicted summarily in magistrates' courts. (It has a very limited civil jurisdiction relating, for example, to licensing appeals.)

(*b*) *Composition.* The judges of the Crown Court are judges of the High Court, circuit judges and recorders. A judge of the court generally sits alone, but may be joined by justices of the peace where the court is hearing proceedings on committal relating to sentence.

22. Queen's Bench Division. The division provides the judges who try the most serious of the criminal offences at the Crown Court. It may also hear appeals in summary criminal cases on points of law by way of case stated from a magistrates' court or the Crown Court. (*See* also **5** above.)

(*a*) *Jurisdiction.* Appeals on points of law. *See*, e.g. Magistrates' Courts Act 1980, s. 111(1).

(*b*) *Composition.* Two to three Queen's Bench Division judges. The Lord Chief Justice may preside.

23. Court of Appeal (Criminal Division). The court replaced the Court of Criminal Appeal under the Criminal Appeal Act 1966. *See* Criminal Appeal Act 1968, S.C.A. 1981, s. 3(1).

(*a*) *Jurisdiction.* The court hears appeals against conviction on indictment where a point of law is involved; hears appeals against a sentence of the Crown Court; and hears appeals by the prosecution against acquittals on a point of law arising out of a trial in the Crown Court.

(*b*) *Composition.* The court consists of the Lord Chief Justice, Lords Justices of Appeal and Queen's Bench Division judges. At least three judges sit to hear an appeal. *See* S.C.A. 1981, ss. 3, 55(4).

24. House of Lords. Appeals, brought by the prosecution or defence, may be heard by Lords of Appeal in Ordinary in the House of Lords where a point of law of general public importance is involved and leave to appeal has been given. (*See also* **12** above.) *See* XI, **5**.

25. Judicial Committee of the Privy Council. The Judicial Committee of the Privy Council considers appeals from criminal courts outside the U.K., e.g. other parts of the Commonwealth. (*See also* **13** above.)

NOTE: The term "Supreme Court" refers to the court created by the Judicature Acts 1873–75, which now comprises the Court of Appeal, the High Court of Justice and the Crown Court: *see* S.C.A. 1981, s. 1(1).

THE DOCTRINE OF STARE DECISIS

26. The concept of stare decisis. The phrase refers to the doctrine according to which certain clauses of judicial precedent must be followed: *see* II, **17–19**. (*Stare decisis et non quieta movere* means to stand by precedents and not to disturb settled points.)

27. Stare decisis and the hierarchy of the courts. The doctrine is reflected in the practice of the courts as follows:

(*a*) *House of Lords.* In *London Street Tramways Co.* v. *L.C.C.* (1898) the House recognised that it was bound by its previous decisions. In 1966, however, the Lord Chancellor announced that, in future, the Lords would depart from their own decisions "when it appears right to do so".

(*b*) *Court of Appeal* (*Civil Division*). The Civil Division is bound by its previous decisions except where a decision is inconsistent with a subsequent House of Lords decision or where a decision has been given *per incuriam*, i.e. where the court has failed to take into account an earlier inconsistent decision of the Lords or itself where there are two conflicting decisions: *see Young* v. *Bristol Aeroplane Co. Ltd.* (1944); *Midland Bank* v. *Hett* (1978).

(*c*) *Court of Appeal* (*Criminal Division*). The court considers itself to be bound generally by its own previous decisions: *see R.* v. *Taylor* (1950); *R* v. *Gould* (1968).

(*d*) *Divisional courts.* In civil matters they are bound by decisions of the House of Lords and the Court of Appeal (Civil Division). In criminal matters the courts appear to be able to depart from earlier decisions; see *R.* v. *Greater Manchester Coroner* (1984).

(*e*) *High Court.* High Court judges are bound by decisions of superior courts, but not by one another's rulings.

(*f*) *Crown Court.* Crown Court judges are apparently bound by decisions of the superior courts, but not by one another's rulings.

(*g*) *Inferior courts.* Magistrates' courts and county courts are bound by the decisions of superior courts.

PERSONNEL OF THE LAW (1)

28. Barristers and solicitors. The legal profession in Britain is divided, in unique fashion, into two separate branches:

(*a*) *Barristers.* Known also as "counsel" and, collectively, as "the Bar". Barristers are "called to the bar" by one of the four Inns of Court (Lincoln's Inn, Gray's Inn, Inner Temple and Middle Temple). Their governing body is the Senate of the Inns of Court and the Bar. Barristers have a right of audience in almost all judicial proceedings. Their tasks include the giving of expert legal opinion to solicitors and their clients and the conduct of cases on behalf of clients in the courts. Queen's Counsel are barristers appointed on the recommendation of the Lord Chancellor.

(*b*) *Solicitors.* Solicitors of the Supreme Court are qualified persons who may conduct legal proceedings in certain courts and advise on legal problems. Solicitors have passed the examinations of the Law Society and possess a certificate allowing them to practise. The Council of the Law Society is responsible for practice rules: see Solicitors Act 1974. A solicitor's right of audience is limited: he may not appear before the House of Lords, for example.

29. Magistrates. Magistrates ("justices of the peace") need not have special qualifications and are unpaid. They are appointed by the Lord Chancellor (usually on the advice of the Lord Lieutenant of a county or an advisory committee). Their retiring age is seventy. *See* Magistrates' Courts Act 1980; Administration of Justice Act 1973, s. 5; Justices of the Peace Act 1979. Magistrates may be removed for incompetence. Stipendiary magistrates are appointed on the recommendation of the Lord Chancellor from solicitors or barristers of seven years' standing (ten years' in the case of London stipendiaries) and they are paid: *see* Justices of the Peace Act 1979, ss. 13–16.

NOTE: Magistrates' clerks are usually lawyers of not less than five years' standing who advise magistrates (at their request) on matters of law, procedure, etc: *see* Justices of the Peace Act 1979, ss. 25–30; Magistrates' Courts Act 1980, s. 141; *Hill* v. *Anderton* (1982).

30. Coroners. Coroners are appointed under the Coroners Acts 1887–1980 from barristers, solicitors and registered medical practitioners of at least five years' standing.

31. Lord Chancellor. The Lord High Chancellor is a lawyer appointed by the Crown on the Prime Minister's advice. He is the principal legal dignitary, head of the judiciary, a member of the Cabinet and speaker of the House of Lords. He may preside over the Lords when it sits as a court of law.

32. Lord Chief Justice. The Lord Chief Justice presides over the Queen's Bench Division and ranks next to the Lord Chancellor in the legal hierarchy. He may preside over the Court of Appeal (Criminal Division) and the divisional court of the Queen's Bench Division. He is appointed by the sovereign on the Prime Minister's advice. *See* S.C.A. 1981, s. 10(3)(*a*).

33. Master of the Rolls. The Master of the Rolls is head of the Court of Appeal (Civil Division). He is appointed by the sovereign on the Prime Minister's advice. *See* S.C.A. 1981, s. 10.

34. President of the Family Division. The President is the head of the division. He is appointed by the sovereign on the Prime Minister's advice.

35. Vice-Chancellor. The Vice-Chancellor acts, in practice, as head of the Chancery Division and is responsible to the Lord Chancellor for the organisation and management of the division's business. *See* S.C.A. 1981, s. 10.

36. Lords of Appeal in Ordinary. The Law Lords are appointed from barristers of fifteen years' experience or two years' experience in high judicial office (usually in the Court of Appeal). They are appointed by the sovereign on the Prime Minister's advice. *See* Appellate Jurisdiction Act 1876, s. 6.

37. Lords Justices of Appeal. They are appointed from High Court judges and generally have at least fifteen years' experience as barristers, or two years' experience in the High Court. They are appointed by the sovereign on the Prime Minister's advice. *See* S.C.A. 1981, s. 10.

38. Puisne judges. High Court judges are generally drawn from circuit judges or from barristers of at least ten years' standing. They are appointed by the sovereign on the advice of the Lord Chancellor. *See* S.C.A. 1981, s. 4(2).

39. Circuit judges. They are appointed from barristers of at least ten years' standing or from recorders of at least three years' standing, by the sovereign on the advice of the Lord Chancellor. *See* Courts Act 1971, s. 16; S.C.A. 1981, s. 8.

40. Recorders. Recorders are appointed from barristers or solicitors of at least ten years' standing, for periods of five years. They are appointed by the sovereign on the advice of the Lord Chancellor. *See* Courts Act 1971, s. 21; S.C.A. 1981, s. 146.

PERSONNEL OF THE LAW (2)

41. Attorney-General. The Attorney-General is the chief law officer of the Crown and head of the English Bar. He represents the Crown in legal proceedings and conducts some Crown prosecutions. "As the guardian of the public interest, the Attorney-General has a special duty in regard to the enforcement of the law ... it is his duty to represent the public interest with complete objectivity and detachment"; *A.-G.* (*ex rel. McWhirter*) v. *I.B.A.* (1973). *See* also *Gouriet* v. *U.P.W.* (1978). He is generally a Queen's Counsel and a member of Parliament and is appointed by the Prime Minister.

42. Solicitor-General. He is the Attorney-General's deputy, a barrister and member of the House of Commons. He is assisted by Junior Counsel to the Treasury.

43. Director of Public Prosecutions. The Director of Public Prosecutions works under the supervision of the Attorney-General. He is usually a barrister or solicitor of at least ten years' standing and undertakes proceedings in cases of murder and other cases of public importance. Some statutes require his consent to a prosecution. He is appointed by the Home Secretary; *See* Prosecution of Offences Act 1979, s. 1. *See Raymond* v. *A.-G.* (1982).

PROGRESS TEST 7

1. What is meant by (*a*) a superior court, (*b*) a court of record?   **(2)**

2. Outline the jurisdiction of the county courts.   **(3)**

3. Outline the jurisdiction of the Queen's Bench Division.   **(5)**

4. Outline the jurisdiction of the Chancery Division.   **(7)**

5. What is the work of the Family Division?   **(9)**

6. Outline the work of the Court of Appeal (Civil Division).   **(11)**

7. What is the function of the House of Lords as a court of appeal?   **(12)**

8. What is the function of the Judicial Committee of the Privy Council?   **(13)**

9. Explain the work of a coroner's court. **(17)**

10. Outline the functions of the magistrates' courts. **(20)**

11. Explain the nature of the Crown Court. **(21)**

12. Explain the work of the Court of Appeal (Criminal Division). **(23)**

13. What is meant by the concept of *stare decisis*? **(26)**

14. What is the work of the Master of the Rolls? How is he appointed? **(33)**

15. How are the Lords Justices of Appeal appointed? **(37)**

16. What is the work of the Attorney-General? **(41)**

17. What is the work of the Director of Public Prosecutions? **(43)**

CHAPTER VIII

The Courts in Action (1): Civil Proceedings

INTRODUCTORY MATTERS

1. Importance of procedure. Procedural forms and patterns are evident in the work of the English courts. In relation to the topics discussed in this chapter, they are based on the County Court Rules 1959 and 1981, as subsequently amended (*see* the "Green Book"— *County Court Practice*) and the Rules of the Supreme Court 1965, as subsequently amended (*see* the "White Book"—*Supreme Court Practice*). *See* also the County Courts Act 1984. It should be noted that the rules are no more than guides to procedure; they do not affect the substantive law. "The Rules of the Supreme Court are the instrument through which the courts act to secure justice, their servants not their tyrants": *per* Oliver J. in *Burston Finance* v. *Wilkins* (1975).

2. Matters to be discussed. Two aspects of civil proceedings are selected for discussion below:

(*a*) procedure in the county courts (*see* **3–7** below);
(*b*) procedure in the Queen's Bench Division (*see* **8–17** below).

PROCEDURE IN THE COUNTY COURTS

3. Choice of court: summons. The plaintiff ("the person asking for relief") is expected to commence proceedings in the court for the district in which the defendant resides or conducts his business or in the court where the cause of action arose wholly or in part. An action is commenced by the plaintiff's filing in the court office a request for a summons, setting out details of the claim, which is served by the plaintiff or the county court bailiff (*see* Ord. 12). The defendant who has been served with a summons may take one of the following courses of action:

(*a*) he may pay the whole or part of the claim into court within fourteen days of service, thus staying the action;
(*b*) he may admit the whole or part of the claim, but ask for time to pay;
(*c*) he may plead a set-off or counter-claim; or
(*d*) he may appear and dispute the plaintiff's claim.

NOTE: The County Court Rules 1981, Ord. 19, rr. 1–6, allow a "small claims" procedure whereby claims based on a statutorily fixed sum, or less, are heard by county courts under a simple, informal procedure.

4. Pre-trial review: settlement. The county court registrar makes a preliminary consideration of the action (see County Court Rules 1981, Ord. 17, r. 1). Evidence may be given on affidavit at the review. Judgment may be entered for the plaintiff if the defendant fails to appear, or does not deliver an admission or defence. Alternatively, the action is determined before the trial if the parties reach a settlement.

5. Trial. In the absence of settlement or discontinuance of the action by the plaintiff, the trial takes place before the judge, or registrar, and—in relatively few cases—with a jury of eight persons (see County Courts Act 1984, s. 67). Judgment is delivered for the plaintiff if the defendant fails to appear or admits the plaintiff's claim.

6. Default actions. Should the plaintiff claim a liquidated demand (i.e. for a fixed sum) or a debt, he must proceed by means of a default action, so that the plaintiff is entitled to enter judgment in default where the defendant has failed to take the necessary steps. (This does not apply in the case of actions in tort, actions brought by a moneylender for debt or interest or actions to recover money secured by a mortgage: see Ord. 83, Ord. 88.) An *interlocutory judgment* leaves the amount due to the plaintiff to be assessed; a *final judgment* states the amount for which defendant is liable.

7. Enforcing the judgment. In the case of a judgment for the payment of money, this may be enforced by execution against the defendant's property, creation of a charge over his land, etc. An execution summons may be issued, directing the bailiff to seize the defendant's personal property so as to satisfy the judgment debt. The defendant's earnings may be attached: see Attachment of Earnings Act 1971, as amended by the Administration of Justice Act 1982, ss. 53–54. Note that county court judgments do not generally carry interest; High Court judgments do.

PROCEDURE IN THE QUEEN'S BENCH DIVISION (1)

8. Commencing an action in the Queen's Bench Division. This may be done by writ or originating summons.

(a) *Writ*, e.g. in case of claim based on allegation of fraud or tort. The writ is a command to the defendant to enter an appearance in the action. It states the parties' names and may be endorsed with a statement of claim. It is "issued" by the plaintiff sending copies to the Central Office or a district registry; once issued, it is valid for twelve months.

(b) *Originating summons*, e.g. where it appears possible to determine the dispute on a point of law. The hearing of the summons is usually before a *master* who may make an order against the defendant, or may order the continuation of proceedings as if a writ had been issued, or may order transfer of the action to an appropriate court, or may "give such directions as to the further conduct of the proceedings [as appear best] to secure the just, expeditious and economical disposal thereof": Ord. 28, r. 4(2). *See also* Ord. 7, r. 2.

9. Appearance. The defendant may acknowledge service of writ and give notice of intention to defend. Should he fail to enter an appearance, the plaintiff may be entitled to final or interlocutory judgment in default of appearance: *See* Ord. 35, r. 1.

10. Staying proceedings; discontinuance; settlement; application for summary judgment. Following appearance, any of the following procedures may result:

(a) *Stay of proceedings*. The court may order a stay where, for example, a party has failed to comply with an order: *see* Ord. 18, Ord. 19.

(b) *Discontinuance*. The plaintiff may serve a notice of discontinuance, indicating that he does not wish to proceed further: *see* Ord. 21.

(c) *Settlement*. The parties may make a settlement of the dispute and, therefore, will withdraw before the formal trial.

(d) *Summary judgment*. Under Ord. 14, in the case of an action in the Queen's Bench Division commenced by writ, *other than* one relating to an allegation of fraud or false imprisonment, libel, slander, malicious prosecution, the plaintiff may issue an "Order 14 summons". If contested, the defendant must attend and show that he has a triable defence. On hearing the summons, the master may give final or interlocutory judgment for the plaintiff, unless the defendant establishes that there is an issue in dispute which ought to be tried or that, for some other reason, there ought to be a trial. He may give the defendant conditional or unconditional leave to defend the action; he may give judgment with a stay of execution pending the trial of a counterclaim; he may transfer the action to a county court.

PROCEDURE IN THE QUEEN'S BENCH DIVISION (2)

11. Pleadings. If the action has not been determined, the parties are obliged to exchange pleadings.

(a) "Every pleading must contain, and contain only, a statement in a summary form of the material facts on which the party pleading relies for his claim or defence, as the case may be, but not the evidence by which those facts are to be proved, and the statement must be as brief as the nature of the case admits": Ord. 18, r. 7(1).

(b) The pleadings must contain facts only and should comprise *all material* facts.

(c) The object of pleadings is to eradicate irrelevant matters, to state issues precisely and to allow the parties time for considered replies.

(d) Where a pleading consists of a statement of claim, it must be dealt with by the defendant so that each allegation is admitted or denied, or admitted in the context of facts which nullify the effect of admittance ("confession and avoidance"): *see* Ord. 18, r. 8(1).

12. Discovery and inspection of documents. A party may disclose to the court or to other parties relevant documents in his possession or power. Notice to inspect documents may be served on an opponent. *See* S.C.A. 1981, ss. 33–35; Ord. 24, r. 10; Ord. 38, r. 13.

13. Interrogatories. Written questions, answerable on oath, relating to any matter relevant to an action, may be administered with leave to an opponent: *see* Ord. 26. The object is to obtain admissions and to limit the scope of an opponent's case. They must be answered within the time prescribed and answers are binding.

14. Summons for directions. Within one month of the close of pleadings the plaintiff must issue a summons for directions, returnable in not less than 14 days: Ord. 25, r. 1. The object is to allow a consideration of trial preparations so that all appropriate matters can be dealt with and to allow directions to be given as to the cause of the action.

15. Trial. Witnesses are named; documents are prepared. If neither party appears when the case is called, the action may be struck off the list. If the defendant fails to appear, and the plaintiff appears, the plaintiff may prove his claim and obtain judgment. If the plaintiff fails to appear, the defendant may be given judgment. Trial is in open court. If there is a jury (*see* **16** below), its members will be sworn. The trial continues in the following manner:

(a) The plaintiff generally opens his case, stating the facts upon which he relies, in relation to the pleadings.

(b) The plaintiff's witnesses are examined, cross-examined and re-examined (*see* X, **8**).

(*c*) Documents and answers to interrogatories are presented.

(*d*) The defendant may submit that there is "no case to answer", i.e. that the plaintiff has not made out a prima facie case. If the submission succeeds, judgment for the defendant is entered; if it fails, the case proceeds (or where the defendant has been asked to "stand on the submission", judgment may be entered for the plaintiff). The defendant may indicate that he does not wish to call any evidence and, in that event, counsel for the plaintiff addresses the court and is followed by the defence counsel.

(*e*) If the case continues, the defence counsel outlines his defence and calls his witnesses. They are examined, cross-examined and re-examined.

(*f*) The defence counsel makes a closing speech.

(*g*) The plaintiff may make a closing speech in reply.

16. Trial by jury. There is a right to trial by jury in an action in the Queen's Bench Division relating to fraud, libel, slander, malicious prosecution or false imprisonment: S.C.A. 1981, s. 69(1). The right may not be exercised, however, if the court is of the opinion that the trial will require a prolonged examination of documents or accounts or any scientific investigation which cannot be made conveniently with a jury: s. 69(1). *See* also Ord. 33, r. 5. In all other cases in the Queen's Bench Division, the judge has a *discretion* to allow trial by jury. That discretion must be exercised judicially; it should be used only exceptionally, e.g. where there is a substantial dispute about facts; its use in personal injury cases should be very rare: see *Ward* v. *James* (1966); *Hodges* v. *Harland & Wolff Ltd.* (1965). "When in a civil case a man's honour or integrity is at stake, or when one or another party must be deliberately lying, then trial by jury has no equal": *per* Lord Denning in *Ward* v. *James* (1966).

17. Verdict and judgment. The judge sums up, stating the legal issues, explaining the appropriate burden and standard of proof (*see* X, **11–12**) to the jury, where there is one. The verdict is given and judgment is entered. Judgment for the payment of money may be enforced (*see* Ord. 45, r. 1) by a charging order; a writ directing the sheriff to seize the debtor's goods; appointment of a receiver; or by a writ of sequestration (by which persons may be directed to enter upon and take possession of the judgment debtor's real and personal estate): Ord. 45, r. 5. Judgment for possession of land may be enforced by a writ of possession. Judgment for delivery of goods may be enforced by a writ of delivery: Ord. 45, r. 4. *See* also Civil Jurisdiction and Judgments Act 1982.

PROGRESS TEST 8

1. What matters affect the choice of a county court for the hearing of an action?   **(3)**

2. What is the pre-trial review?   **(4)**

3. Explain the nature of a default action in relation to county court procedure.   **(6)**

4. Explain the nature of a writ issued in relation to Queen's Bench Division proceedings.   **(8)**

5. How does a defendant "enter an appearance"?   **(9)**

6. Explain summary judgment under Ord. 14.   **(10)**

7. What are "pleadings"?   **(11)**

8. What are "interrogatories"?   **(13)**

9. Explain the object of a summons for directions.   **(14)**

10. Outline the procedure at a trial in the Queen's Bench Division.   **(15)**

11. How is a judgment for the payment of money enforced?   **(17)**

CHAPTER IX

The Courts in Action (2): Criminal Proceedings

INTRODUCTORY MATTERS

1. Importance of procedure. Procedure in the criminal courts reflects some very important basic principles in English criminal law: the accused is presumed innocent until his guilt is proved beyond reasonable doubt (*see* X, **12**(*b*)); the interest of the Crown is that the right person must be convicted, so that the prosecution should urge neither conviction nor punishment. Procedure is accusatorial (*see* III, **27**) so that the judge in criminal proceedings acts as umpire; he will question the accused only to clarify ambiguities, etc.

2. Matters to be discussed. The following points are touched upon in this chapter:

(*a*) procedure at committal proceedings (*see* **3–5** below);

(*b*) section 1 committals (*see* **6** below);

(*c*) procedure at summary trials (*see* **7–8** below);

(*d*) procedure at trial on indictment (*see* **9–17** below).

COMMITTAL PROCEEDINGS

3. Essence of committal proceedings. Before a person can be tried on indictment (by a jury) he must be brought before one or more magistrates so that a preliminary examination may be conducted. The task of the magistrates is not to determine the case; it is solely to determine whether there is evidence on which a prima facie case can be made out. *See* Magistrates' Courts Act 1980, ss. 4–8.

4. Procedure (1). The following pattern is usually followed:

(*a*) The prosecution calls witnesses who present evidence under oath.

(*b*) Witnesses may be cross-examined by the accused and his counsel/solicitor and may be re-examined by the prosecution.

(*c*) Witnesses' evidence is reduced to written form by the magistrates' clerk and is known as a "deposition".

(*d*) Depositions are read out to witnesses in the presence of the accused and signed, and attested by the magistrates' clerk.

(*e*) The accused may submit that there is "no case to answer", and that the charge ought to be dismissed.

(*f*) If the charge is not dismissed it is written down and read, and explained, to the accused.

5. Procedure (2). The pattern of procedure continues as follows:

(*a*) The accused is asked if he wishes to say anything in answer to the charge. His rights, for example, to give evidence on oath, are explained to him.

(*b*) What the accused says is written down and read to him.

(*c*) The accused is given the opportunity of presenting evidence on oath and calling witnesses.

(*d*) The accused and witnesses are cross-examined and re-examined.

(*e*) The counsel/solicitor for the accused may address the court once again.

(*f*) If the court decides that there is a prima facie case to answer, the accused is committed for trial; if not, the accused is discharged, i.e. set free after the charge is dismissed.

6. Section 1 committal. Under the Criminal Justice Act 1967, s. 1, the accused may be committed for trial without consideration of the evidence, where the entire evidence for the prosecution and defence is in *written form* and where the accused has legal representation. *See* Magistrates' Courts Act 1980, ss. 6(2), 102. The procedure is as follows:

(*a*) The charge is written down and read to the accused.

(*b*) The accused is asked if he objects to any of the written evidence, if he wishes to give evidence or call witnesses or if he intends to submit that there is no case to answer.

(*c*) If the accused wishes to take any of these courses of action, proceedings will continue as ordinary proceedings.

(*d*) If the accused does not wish to take any of these courses of action, the written statements of evidence are received by the court.

(*e*) The accused is told to provide details of any alibi on which he intends to rely. (Note: an "alibi" is a defence whereby the accused alleges that at the supposed time of commission of the offence he was elsewhere.)

(*f*) The accused is then committed for trial without consideration of the contents of the written evidence.

SUMMARY TRIAL

7. Essence of summary trial. Summary trial is concerned with offences, details of which are heard before magistrates and without a jury.

8. Procedure. The following pattern of procedure is observed:

(*a*) The accused is asked by the clerk whether he pleads guilty or not guilty. A plea of guilty is generally followed by conviction without evidence being heard: Magistrates' Courts Act 1980, s. 9.

(*b*) Following a plea of not guilty, the prosecution opens its case and calls witnesses who are examined, cross-examined and re-examined.

(*c*) The defence may submit that there is no case to answer. If accepted, the case is dismissed; if rejected, the case continues.

(*d*) The accused or his representative addresses the court.

(*e*) The defence evidence is called.

(*f*) Evidence in rebuttal may be called by the prosecution.

(*g*) If both parties have made opening addresses, the prosecution, then the defence, will address the court.

(*h*) The magistrates retire, consider their verdict and pass sentence, or dismiss the charge.

NOTE: Under the Magistrates' Courts Act 1980, s. 12, the accused may plead guilty to an offence triable only summarily, without attending court. (The prosecution need not attend, since the accused has admitted the facts.)

TRIAL ON INDICTMENT (1)

9. Essence of indictment. An indictment is a written accusation of a crime, drawn up in accordance with the Indictments Act 1915 and Indictments Rules 1971. An (imaginary) example is as follows:

The Crown Court at Chester
The Queen *v*. A.B.
A.B. is charged as follows:
Statement of offence: Theft, contrary to s. 1 of the Theft Act 1968.
Particulars of offence: A.B. on the 10th day of May 1977, in the City of Chester, stole ten bottles of wine, the property of C.D.
      Signed (by the Officer of the Crown Court).

10. Arraignment and plea. The accused is called to the bar of the court by the clerk and the indictment is read. After each count (i.e. offence) is read, the accused is asked whether he pleads guilty or not guilty. He may make a plea of *autrefois acquit* or *autrefois convict* (i.e. that he has been tried and acquitted or convicted of the offence on a previous occasion) or he may stand mute when asked to plead (in which case a plea of not guilty may be entered for him). He may plead guilty or not guilty. If he pleads guilty, the prosecution gives the facts, evidence of character and pleas in mitigation are heard and sentence is passed. If he pleads not guilty, the trial proceeds.

11. The jury. The jury has been picked from persons registered as electors, aged eighteen to sixty-five, who have been resident in the U.K. for at least five years since the age of thirteen: *see* Juries Act 1974, s. 1. Under the 1974 Act certain classes of persons are *ineligible* for jury service, for example, lawyers, police officers, ministers of religion and persons who are mentally handicapped; members of Parliament, medical practitioners and serving soldiers, for example, may be *excused* from service if they wish; among those *disqualified* from jury service are persons who have been imprisoned within the last ten years or who have, at any time, been sentenced to five years or more imprisonment.

(*a*) The jury is sworn.

(*b*) The accused may challenge (without disclosing the cause) up to three jurors (Criminal Law Act 1977, s. 12), or he may challenge (for cause) the entire jury.

12. Case for the prosecution. Counsel for the prosecution generally opens the case, states the facts on which he intends to rely and calls witnesses. They are examined, cross-examined and re-examined by the defence counsel and re-examined by the prosecuting counsel.

13. "No case to answer". The defence may submit that there is no case to answer. The defence may address the court and the prosecuting counsel may reply. The judge may accept the submission and direct the jury to return a verdict of not guilty. If not, the case continues. *See R.* v. *Galbraith* (1981).

TRIAL ON INDICTMENT (2)

14. Case for the defence. The procedure varies in accordance with the accused being represented by counsel or not. It also depends on whether evidence other than that of the accused himself and witnesses as to character is adduced. *See* Criminal Evidence Act 1898, s. 2.

(*a*) Where evidence is to be adduced other than that of the defendant himself and witnesses only as to character:

    (*i*) the defendant, or his counsel, may open the defence;

    (*ii*) defence witnesses (including the defendant, if he wishes to give evidence) will then be examined;

    (*iii*) the prosecuting counsel will sum up the evidence on behalf of the prosecution;

(*iv*) the defendant (or his counsel) will sum up evidence for the defence.

(*b*) Where no evidence is adduced save that of the defendant himself and witnesses as to character, and the defendant is not represented by counsel:

(*i*) the defendant, if he wishes, will give his evidence and witnesses as to character will give their evidence;

(*ii*) the defendant will address the jury.

(*c*) Where no evidence is adduced save that of the defendant himself and witnesses as to character, and the defendant is represented by counsel:

(*i*) the defendant may give his evidence, and witnesses as to character will give their evidence;

(*ii*) the prosecuting counsel will sum up his case;

(*iii*) the defending counsel will sum up his case.

15. Rebutting evidence, and calling of witnesses by the judge. In general, the prosecution may not call further evidence after the close of the case for the prosecution. The judge has a discretionary power to allow further evidence introduced by the defence which could not have been foreseen by the prosecution. The judge may call a witness not called by either side, and without the consent of either side, if he considers it necessary in the interests of justice: *see R. v. Harris* (1927); *R. v. Oliva* (1965).

16. Closing speeches. Following the summing-up of evidence by the prosecution, counsel for the accused sums up the case for the defence. The rule is that the defence has the right to the last word: *see* Criminal Procedure (Right of Reply) Act 1964.

17. Summing up, verdict and sentence. Following the closing speeches, the trial reaches its final stages.

(*a*) The judge sums up. He directs on the points of law involved, reviews the evidence given and directs as to burden and standard of proof.

(*b*) The jury retires and returns to announce its verdict, through its chosen foreman, in open court. The verdict need not be unanimous if, in a case where there are not less than eleven jurors, ten of them agree on the verdict, or in a case where there are ten jurors, nine of them agree on the verdict. A majority verdict is not accepted unless it appears to the court that the jury have had not less than two hours or so for deliberation (or longer, if the court thinks reasonable) and unless the foreman states in open court the number of jurors who agreed to the verdict: *see* Juries Act 1974, s. 17. Where the jury fails to agree on a verdict (or if there are three or more in the minority) they will be discharged and a new jury will be called to try the case. Should there be another disagreement, the prosecution will not generally offer evidence in a third trial, so that the accused is then acquitted.

(c) Following a verdict of guilty, the accused is asked if he has anything to say before sentence is passed. Pleas in mitigation are heard and sentence is given orally by the judge. Sentence may take the form of imprisonment, suspended sentence or fine (in lieu of, or in addition to, other penalties): *see* Powers of Criminal Courts Act 1973.

PROGRESS TEST 9

1. Outline the pattern of procedure in committal proceedings. **(4, 5)**

2. What is a "section 1 committal"? **(6)**

3. Outline procedure in a summary trial. **(8)**

4. What is an indictment? **(9)**

5. Explain the nature of arraignment and plea. **(10)**

6. Explain the phrase "no case to answer". **(13)**

7. Outline procedure relating to the case for the defence in a trial on indictment. **(14)**

8. What is a "majority verdict"? **(17)**

CHAPTER X

The Law of Evidence

INTRODUCTORY MATTERS

1. The importance of evidence in our legal system. The rules governing admissibility of evidence and the modes of proving facts are of much importance in our law of procedure. What may be said in evidence, by whom, in what manner: these matters are controlled carefully by the court. Rules of evidence grew in importance as the jury system developed and as attempts intensified to prevent untrained juries from being misled by false witnesses. The accusatorial system (*see* III, **27**) makes the adducing and style of evidence of considerable importance.

2. Definition. Evidence may be defined as the legally admissible facts into which the court will enquire, the legal means of attempting to prove or disprove those facts before the court, and the resulting body of rules of law attaching thereto. In essence, evidence is, in Blackstone's words: "that which demonstrates, makes clear or ascertains the truth of the very fact or point in issue, either on the one side or on the other".

3. Types of evidence. Among the more important types of evidence are the following:

(*a*) *Direct evidence* (i.e. a testimony concerning a fact actually perceived by a witness with his own senses) and *hearsay evidence* (i.e. evidence of some fact not actually perceived by a witness with his own senses, but proved by him to have been the subject of a statement by some other person): *see* **27–30** below.

(*b*) *Circumstantial evidence* (i.e. evidence of a fact not in issue, but relevant to a fact in issue, from which some fact in issue can be inferred): *see*, e.g., *R.* v. *Dalloz* (1908).

(*c*) *Oral evidence* (i.e. a witness's testimony given by word of mouth in the witness box) and *documentary evidence* (i.e. evidence derived by the court from the inspection of documents).

(*d*) *Real evidence* (i.e. evidence derived by the court from the inspection of physical objects, other than documents, made available for inspection).

4. Functions of the judge and the jury in relation to evidence. In general, matters of *law* arising during proceedings fall to be determined by the *judge*; matters of *fact*, by the *jury*: *see Mechanical Inventions* v. *Austin* (1935). Thus, in a case of libel (*see* XVI, **25**) it falls to the judge to decide whether certain words are capable of bearing a defamatory meaning; it is for the jury, however, to decide whether, in fact, those words did bear that meaning: *see Nevill* v. *Fine Art Co.* (1897).

WITNESSES

5. Preliminary matters. A witness is one who gives evidence at a hearing. His testimony is his statement in court, offered as the truth of that which he asserts. The following matters relating to witnesses are touched upon below:

(*a*) competency (*see* **6** below);

(*b*) compellability (*see* **7** below);

(*c*) sworn and unsworn evidence and examination of witnesses (*see* **8** below);

(*d*) corroboration (*see* **9** below).

6. The competency of witnesses. Evidence must be given by legally competent witnesses and, in general, all persons are competent as witnesses in judicial proceedings. There are, however, some exceptions to this general rule, for example:

(*a*) Persons of defective intellect are not generally competent (save during a lucid interval).

(*b*) A child who, in the opinion of the court, cannot understand the nature and consequence of an oath, may not give evidence in civil proceedings. In criminal proceedings there is statutory power which allows a child of tender years to give unsworn testimony if he has sufficient intelligence and comprehends the duty of speaking truthfully.

(*c*) The accused person is generally incompetent as a witness for the prosecution: see also *Police and Criminal Evidence Act* 1984, s. 80.

7. The compellability of witnesses. In general, those who are competent witnesses are also compellable to give evidence. There may be exceptions in the case of the accused, or the spouse of the accused: see also *Police and Criminal Evidence Act* 1984, s. 80.

8. Sworn and unsworn evidence and examination of witnesses. Evidence must generally be given on oath. Those who object to being sworn may "affirm", i.e. they make a solemn declaration. In some cases (for example, involving children of tender years) unsworn evidence may be given. Witnesses are subject to the following types of examination:

(*a*) *Examination-in-chief*. Object: the placing of a witness's story before the court so as to obtain a testimony in support of the facts which the party calling that witness is suggesting as true.

(*b*) *Cross-examination*. Object: the eliciting of information concerning facts in issue favourable to the party on whose behalf it is conducted and the throwing of doubt on the accuracy of evidence given against that party.

(*c*) *Re-examination*. Object: the demonstration of a more favourable meaning of the evidence arising in the cross-examination. *See* Civil Evidence Act 1968, s. 2.

9. Corroboration. Corroboration is independent, admissible evidence tending to confirm that some item of principal evidence is true. ("Perhaps the best synonym is 'support'": *D.P.P.* v. *Hester* (1972)). *See R.* v. *Baskerville* (1916); *D.P.P.* v. *Kilbourne* (1973). It may be required:

(*a*) *as a matter of law*, for example, under the Perjury Act 1911, s. 13, or in a charge of treason (*see* Treason Act 1795, s. 1);

(*b*) *as a matter of practice*, for example, in the case of an allegation of a matrimonial offence, or in the case of claims against the estate of a deceased person: *see Re Cummins* (1972).

PROOF

10. Preliminary matters. The term "proof" is used in the law of evidence in a very special sense: it refers to those methods by which the existence or non-existence of facts is established to the satisfaction of the court. The following matters are mentioned below:

(*a*) burden of proof (*onus probandi*) (*see* **11** below);

(*b*) standard of proof required (*see* **12** below);

(*c*) documentary evidence (*see* **13** below).

11. The burden of proof. This phrase refers to the obligation resting on a party to prove his case by proving the facts in issue. Thus, if X is charged with murdering Y, the burden of proving X's unlawful killing of Y, with malice aforethought (*see* XIII, **4**(*c*)) rests on the prosecution (*see* III, **22**). In a civil case, the burden of proof lies "on he who affirms, not upon the person who denies"; hence the plaintiff must prove all those facts which are essential elements in his cause of action.

12. The standard of proof. The general rules are as follows:

(*a*) *In civil cases*, the standard of proof is "proof on a preponderance of probability". "If the evidence is such that the tribunal can say 'we think it more probable than not', the burden is discharged, but if the probabilities are equal it is not"; *per* Denning J. in *Miller* v. *Minister of Pensions* (1947). *See Hornal* v. *Neuberger Products Ltd.* (1957).

(*b*) *In criminal cases*, the standard of proof is "proof beyond reasonable doubt". "If the evidence is so strong against a man as to leave only a remote possibility in his favour, which can be dismissed with the sentence 'of course it is possible but not in the least probable' the case is proved beyond reasonable doubt, but nothing short of that will suffice": *per* Denning J. in *Miller* v. *Minister of Pensions* (1947). *See R.* v. *Summers* (1952).

13. Documentary evidence. In general, the party producing a document must prove the *contents* of the document (by producing it, for example) and the *validity or due execution* of that document. In some cases extrinsic evidence may be given, for example, to show that a document is invalid because of circumstances such as duress or mistake: *see Murray* v. *Parker* (1854).

(*a*) In some cases, secondary evidence of a document may be given, for example, where the original is lost, or its production is very inconvenient. Under the Civil Evidence Act 1968, there are important provisions relating to documentary evidence.

(*b*) Under the Evidence Act 1938, s. 4, there is a presumption (*see* **17** below) that, in the case of civil or criminal proceedings, a document not less than twenty years old has been validly executed.

(*c*) A document is presumed to have been executed on the date stated therein.

MATTERS OF WHICH PROOF IS NOT REQUIRED

14. Preliminary matters. In some cases facts need not be proved by evidence, i.e. having been asserted, they do not require any affirmative proof. Three of these matters are considered below:

(*a*) facts admitted formally (*see* **15** below);

(*b*) facts of which the court takes judicial notice (*see* **16** below);

(*c*) facts which may be presumed in favour of some party (*see* **17–19** below).

15. Facts admitted formally. Formal admissions made in a *civil case* on the pleadings, or during the trial do not generally require proof. Formal admissions in *criminal proceedings* made by or on behalf of prosecution or accused may be made at the trial: *see* Criminal Justice Act 1967, s. 10. *See R.* v. *Lennard* (1973).

16. Facts of which the court takes judicial notice. Where a fact is widely or commonly known, there may be no need to consider formal evidence as to its existence or nature. Four groups of facts which are generally the object of judicial notice are:

(*a*) matters of common and certain knowledge;

(*b*) matters of law, procedure and custom;

(*c*) matters relating to constitutional, political and administrative affairs;

(*d*) official seals and signatures of judges.

17. Presumptions (1). A presumption is an assumption which may or must be made and maintained until evidence to the contrary is given. The first, important group of such presumptions is known as *irrebuttable presumptions of law*, i.e. inferences which the law will not permit any evidence to be called to contradict. Example: the presumption that a child under ten cannot have a guilty intention. In its effect, a presumption of this type is a rule of substantive law.

18. Presumptions (2). A second group is known as *rebuttable presumptions of law*. These are conclusive until disproved by evidence to the contrary. Examples: every person is presumed sane until the contrary be proved; a child born to parents married to each other is presumed to be their legitimate child: *see Gardner* v. *Gardner* (1877).

19. Presumptions (3). A third group is known as *rebuttable presumptions of fact*, i.e. inferences which may be drawn, but there is no compulsion as to this. Example: there is a presumption that a person intends the natural consequences of his acts. *See* Law of Property Act 1925, s. 184.

MATTERS OF WHICH PROOF IS NOT ALLOWED

20. Preliminary matters. In some cases the rules of evidence operate so as to exclude proof. Two matters relating to circumstances in which proof is not allowed are mentioned below:

(*a*) estoppel (*see* **21** below);

(*b*) privilege (*see* **22–23** below).

21. Estoppel. Estoppel is a rule of evidence, the application of which may result in a party's being prohibited from asserting or denying some fact.

(*a*) Estoppel by *record* prohibits a person from raising an allegation previously decided against him by a court of competent jurisdiction: *see Re May* (1885).

(*b*) Estoppel by *deed* usually arises on the rule that a person who is a party to a deed or instrument under seal may neither dispute nor deny its contents *see Baker* v. *Dewey* (1823).

(*c*) Estoppel by *conduct* arises where "one by his conduct or words unlawfully causes another to believe in the existence of a certain state of things, and induces him to act on that belief, or to alter his own previous position, the former is concluded from averring against the latter a different state of things existing at that time": *Pickard* v. *Sears* (1837). *See Taylor Fashions* v. *Liverpool Victoria Trustee Ltd.* (1981).

22. Privilege (1). Privilege attaches to some person so that he has the right to decline to answer certain types of questions. Examples: privilege arising on grounds of public policy (e.g. where disclosure of some fact would prejudice the public interest: *see Duncan* v. *Cammell, Laird & Co. Ltd.* (1942); *Conway* v. *Rimmer* (1968)); privilege relating to matters concerning the detection of crime (*see Rogers* v. *Home Secretary* (1973)); privilege relating to discussions in the jury box or jury room (*see Boston* v. *Bagshaw* (1966)); privilege in relation to written complaint against police under Police Act 1964, s. 49 (*see Conerney* v. *Jacklin* (1985)).

23. Privilege (2). In some circumstances a witness may justifiably refuse to answer questions or interrogatories (*see* VIII, **13**) or produce documents. He may claim, for example, legal professional privilege (e.g. existing between lawyer and client), or he may refuse to answer a question which would involve him in the possibility of facing a criminal charge: *see Re Duncan* (1968).

MATTERS WHICH MAY BE PROVED

24. Preliminary matters. In order to be receivable, evidence must be relevant and admissible. Not all relevant evidence is necessarily admissible. The following matters are mentioned below:

(*a*) facts in issue (*see* **25** below);

(*b*) facts relevant to the issue (*see* **26** below).

25. Facts in issue. These are the facts necessary in order to prove or disprove, to establish or refute, a case. The phrase *res gestae* is used to describe all those facts which comprise, accompany or explain a *transaction* (i.e. the subsidiary facts of which a fact in issue is made up). These may include facts relating to acts done by the accused or by any person in his presence or acting under his direction, and all the statements made by the accused or by a person in his presence at the time of the transaction, or before or after it: *See R.* v. *Sims* (1946).

26. Facts relevant to the issue. These are facts which make probable the existence or non-existence of some fact in issue (or some other relevant fact). They may include: facts probative of a fact in issue; facts tending to show identity of a party; facts showing a state of mind; similar facts. Evidence of "similar facts" is that which is adduced in an attempt to suggest, through its striking similarity, that there is an underlying link between the matters with which it purports to deal – which relate essentially to occasions other than those specifically in question—and the matter now being considered by the court. *See*, for example, *R.* v. *Mortimer* (1936).

HEARSAY

27. Preliminary matters. Hearsay evidence in its legal sense "is evidence given by a testifying witness of a statement made on some other occasion when it is intended as evidence of the truth of what was asserted": *Halsbury's Laws* (4th edn.). Example: X, a witness, may speak only of those facts which he has perceived with any of his senses; he may *not* repeat words spoken by Y with the intention of proving the truth of what Y stated.

28. The hearsay rule. Oral or written statements made by persons who are neither parties nor witnesses are generally inadmissible to prove the truth of the matters contained in these statements. *See R.* v. *Gibson* (1887); *Sparks* v. *R.* (1964); *Jones* v. *Metcalfe* (1967); *R.* v. *Patel* (1981).

29. Exceptions to the rule in civil proceedings. Under the Civil Evidence Act 1968, a hearsay statement in civil proceedings is admissible only by agreement of the parties or under statute or rule of court. The Act preserves, however, some common law exceptions to the hearsay rule, for example, relating to reputation and family tradition, informal admissions, statements in public or official documents.

30. Exceptions to the rule in criminal proceedings. The main exceptions are based on common law sources and statutory provisions. Thus, statements made by deceased persons against interest or in the course of duty may be admitted (*see Taylor* v. *Witham* (1876)). Some further exceptions are: a victim's dying declaration relating to the cause of his death and made "in the settled, hopeless expectation" of death may be admissible (*see R.* v. *Woodcock* (1789); *R.* v. *Perry* (1909)); a confession may be admitted against the party making it if it was voluntary, "in the sense that it has not been obtained from him either by fear of prejudice or hope of advantage held out by a person in authority": *Ibrahim* v. *R.* (1914). *See also* Criminal Evidence Act 1965, s. 1(1).

PROGRESS TEST 10

1. Define evidence. **(2)**
2. What is meant by circumstantial evidence? **(3)**
3. What is the general rule relating to competency and compellability of witnesses? **(6, 7)**
4. What is the meaning of "corroboration"? **(9)**
5. What is the standard of proof required in a criminal case? **(12)**
6. Of what facts will the court take judicial notice? **(16)**
7. Enumerate and illustrate the three main types of presumption. **(17–19)**
8. What is estoppel? **(21)**
9. May privilege arise on grounds of public policy? **(22)**
10. Define facts in issue and facts relevant to the issue. **(25, 26)**
11. State the hearsay rule. **(28)**
12. What are the principal exceptions to the hearsay rule in criminal proceedings? **(30)**

CHAPTER XI

Appeals

INTRODUCTORY MATTERS

1. Right of Appeal. Appeal was defined in *Edlesten* v. *L.C.C.* (1918) as "the transference of a case from an inferior to a higher tribunal in the hope of reversing or modifying the decision of the former": *per* Sankey J. In general there is no right of appeal unless authorised by statute. "It is most elementary that no appeal from a court lies to any other court unless there is a statutory provision which gives the right of appeal. The decision of every court is final, if it has jurisdiction, unless an appeal is given by statute": *per* Lord Goddard in *R.* v. *West Kent Quarter Sessions Appeals Committee, ex parte Files* (1951). Note that a person may not be deprived of a right of appeal given in express terms by statute.

2. Matters to be discussed. Appeals in the civil courts and appeals in the criminal courts are outlined below.

CIVIL APPEALS

3. Preliminary matters. Rights of appeal were derived from the Judicature Acts 1873–75, but in recent years further legislation has extended those rights: *see*, for example, the "leapfrog procedure", outlined in **6** below. *See* Fig. 2 for an outline of appeal procedure in the civil courts.

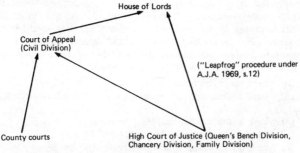

FIG. 2   *Outline of appeal procedure in the civil courts*

4. Appeal to the Court of Appeal (Civil Division). The Court of Appeal (see VII, **11**) is empowered to hear appeals directly from courts below (*see* Supreme Court Act 1981, s. 15). In some cases appeal lies to the High Court and thence to the Court of Appeal. In some circumstances leave to appeal may be required (*see* VII, **11**). Right of appeal may be excluded, for example, from a decision which by statute is considered as final, or in the case of a statute which provides that there is to be no appeal without leave and such leave has been refused.

5. Appeal to the House of Lords. With leave of the Court of Appeal or the House of Lords, appeal lies from the Court of Appeal to the Lords. There is no appeal where statute declares a decision of the Court of Appeal to be final: *see* e.g. County Courts Act 1984, s. 82. *See* VII, **12**.

6. Leapfrog procedure. Under the Administration of Justice Act 1969, s. 12, appeal *direct* from the High Court or a Divisional Court to the House of Lords is possible, without prior appeal to the Court of Appeal, subject to the grant of a certificate by the trial judge and be leave of the House of Lords in a case in which appeal lies to the Court of Appeal. A certificate is not granted unless the parties consent *and* the case involves a point of law of general public importance concerning the construction of some enactment or concerning a point arising from a binding precedent of the Court of Appeal or House of Lords. *See American Cyanamid Co.* v. *Upjohn Co.* (1970).

7. Powers of the Court of Appeal (Civil Division). The Court of Appeal has the power to examine trial witnesses and to receive further evidence orally or by affidavit. "First, it must be shown that the evidence could not have been obtained with reasonable diligence for use at the trial; secondly, the evidence must be such that, if given, it would probably have an important influence on the result of the case, though it need not be decisive; thirdly, the evidence must be such as is presumably to be believed, or, in other words, it must be apparently credible though it need not be incontrovertible": *per* Lord Denning in *Ladd* v. *Marshall* (1954). The court hears appeals on points of law, against findings of fact, against awards of damages, etc. It may order a new trial in the following cases, for example:

    (*a*) where there has been a misdirection of the jury;

    (*b*) where a question has been wrongfully withdrawn from the jury;

    (*c*) where a jury verdict has been perverse;

    (*d*) where a judgment has been obtained by fraud;

    (*e*) where fresh evidence has been discovered: *see Skone* v. *Skone* (1971). *See* also Supreme Court Act 1981, s. 18.

CRIMINAL APPEALS

8. Preliminaries. Matters to be touched upon below include appeal following summary trial and trial on indictment (*see* XII, **4** for explanation of these terms). *See* Fig. 3 for an outline of appeal procedure in the criminal courts.

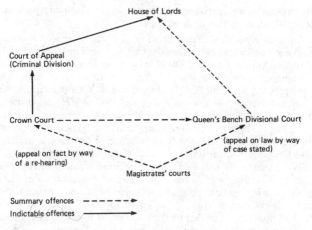

FIG. 3 *Outline of appeal procedure in the criminal courts.*

9. Appeal following summary trial. A person convicted by a magistrates' court may appeal to the Crown Court or to the Queen's Bench Division and thence, in some few cases, to the House of Lords.

(*a*) *Appeal to the Crown Court.* A person who did not plead guilty, and is convicted, may appeal against sentence or conviction or both to the Crown Court. One who pleaded guilty and was convicted may appeal against sentence only. *See* Magistrates' Courts Act 1980, s. 108(1); Supreme Court Act 1981, s. 48.

(*b*) *Appeal to the Queen's Bench Division.* A person convicted may apply to the magistrates' court to state a case for the opinion of a Divisional Court of the Queen's Bench Division. The magistrates' decision may be amended, reversed or affirmed, or remitted to them with the opinion of the Divisional Court. A re-trial cannot be ordered. *See* Magistrates' Courts Act 1980, s. 111.

NOTE: The Crown Court is empowered to state a case for the opinion of the High Court. Either party to a decision of the Crown Court may apply for a case to be stated on the grounds that the decision was in excess of jurisdiction, or was incorrect in law

(*c*) *Appeal to the House of Lords.* Appeal may be made from the Divisional Court if that court grants a certificate stating that a point of law of general public importance has arisen. The House of Lords or the Divisional Court may grant leave to appeal. *See* Administration of Justice Act 1960, s.1.

10. Appeal following trial on indictment. *See* the Criminal Appeal Act 1968, which gives this right of appeal.

(*a*) *Appeal from the Crown Court to the Court of Appeal.* A person convicted on indictment before the Crown Court may appeal to the Court of Appeal (Criminal Division) without leave, against his conviction, on a question of law. With leave of the Court of Appeal, he can appeal against sentence if not fixed by law: Criminal Appeal Act 1968, s. 9. Under the Criminal Justice Act 1972, s. 36(1), the prosecution has a right of appeal on a point of law following an acquittal on indictment. The Court of Appeal may quash a conviction; substitute an alternative verdict; receive fresh evidence; or order a new trial. *See* also Criminal Justice Act 1982; *R.* v. *Rose and Others* (1982).

(*b*) *Appeal to the House of Lords.* The prosecution or defence may appeal to the House of Lords if the Court of Appeal certifies that a point of law of general public importance has arisen *and* the House of Lords or Court of Appeal gives leave to appeal. There is no appeal to the Lords from a refusal by the lower court to certify that a point of law of general public importance is involved. *See* Criminal Appeal Act 1968, s. 33.

(*c*) "The Attorney-General may, if he desires the opinion of the Court of Appeal on a point of law which has arisen in the case, refer that point to the court, and the court shall, in accordance with this section, consider the point and give their opinion on it": Criminal Justice Act 1972, s. 36(1).

11. Applying the proviso. The Court of Appeal or House of Lords, in considering an appeal against conviction, may dismiss an appeal even though satisfied that a point raised should be decided in favour of the appellant, if they consider that no miscarriage of justice has actually occurred. This is known as "applying the proviso": Criminal Appeal Act 1968, proviso to s. 2(1). Example of use of the proviso: *D.P.P.* v. *Morgan* (1975).

PROGRESS TEST 11

1. What is meant by an appeal? **(1)**

2. Can a party appeal to the Court of Appeal (Civil Division) directly from a court below? **(4)**

3. What is the place of the House of Lords in the structure of civil appeals? **(5)**

4. Explain the "leapfrog procedure". **(6)**

5. What are the powers of the Court of Appeal (Civil Division)? **(7)**

6. Explain the appeal procedure following summary trial. **(9)**

7. Explain the appeal procedure following trial on indictment. **(10)**

8. What is meant by "applying the proviso"? **(11)**

CHAPTER XII

Criminal Law (1): Essence of Crime; Responsibility; Defences; Conspiracy and Attempt

INTRODUCTORY MATTERS

1. Nature of criminal law. Criminal law is concerned with matters arising from:

(a) the constituents of a criminal offence;

(b) the proof required so as to establish the facts of such an offence;

(c) the existence of culpability, and its degree, on the part of the offender;

(d) the procedures necessary to establish culpability;

(e) the types of penalty to be imposed as punishment for such an offence.

2. Definition of a crime. The following definitions should be noted:

(a) "A violation of the public rights and duties due to the whole community considered as a community": Blackstone.

(b) "An act that is capable of being followed by criminal proceedings, having one of the types of outcome (punishment, etc.) known to follow those proceedings": Williams.

(c) "An unlawful act or default which is an offence against the public and renders the person guilty of the act liable to legal punishment": *Halsbury's Laws* (adopted as a correct definition by the House of Lords in *Board of Trade* v. *Owen* (1957)).

3. Criminal law and social change. *See* I, 7. Criminal law has evolved as society has evolved and, therefore, mirrors social change. Thus, the introduction of the defence of diminished responsibility (*see* XIII, 6(a)), the abolition of the death penalty in 1964, and the Abortion Act 1967, exemplify some of society's changing attitudes to certain types of conduct. Social attitudes to moral questions are reflected very clearly in changes in the criminal law.

4. Classification of criminal offences. Offences may be classified in a variety of ways, e.g. by relation to subject matter (offences against the person, state or property). More important classifications are as follows:

(*a*) *Arrestable and non-arrestable offences.* Arrestable offences are, under the Criminal Law Act 1967, those "for which the sentence is fixed by law or for which a person (not previously convicted) may under or by virtue of any enactment be sentenced to imprisonment for a term of five years": s. 2(1). An offence may be declared by statute to be "arrestable" although the maximum period of imprisonment is less than five years. All other offences are generally all non-arrestable: *see* also Police and Criminal Evidence Act 1984, s. 116.

(*b*) *Indictable, summary and triable either way.* Under the Criminal Law Act 1977, Part III, offences are classified, for purposes of the mode of trial, as follows:

(*i*) *Indictable offences*: those which, if committed by an adult, are triable on indictment, whether exclusively so triable, or triable either way: s. 64(1)(*a*).

(*ii*) *Summary offences*: those which, if committed by an adult, are triable only summarily: s. 64(1)(*b*).

(*iii*) *Offences triable either way*: those which, if committed by an adult, are triable either on indictment or summarily: s. 64(1)(*c*). *See* Magistrates' Courts Act 1980, ss. 18, 22.

NOTE: The distinction between *felonies* and *misdemeanours* disappeared under the Criminal Law Act 1967, s. 1.

5. Matters to be discussed. The following matters are mentioned in this chapter:

(*a*) problems of criminal responsibility (*see* **6–8** below);
(*b*) general defences to crime (*see* **9–15** below);
(*c*) conspiracy (*see* **16** below);
(*d*) attempt (*see* **17** below).

CRIMINAL RESPONSIBILITY

6. Preliminary matters. The fact that a person's act or omission results in a state of affairs which the law seeks to prevent does not invariably result in criminal responsibility attaching to that person. Consider, for example, the following events in relation to the responsibility of X:

(*a*) X, intending only to frighten and not to harm Y, alarms the horse on which Y is riding, so that Y falls and is killed;
(*b*) X, acting under the insane delusion that Y intends to kill him, shoots Y so as to prevent this;
(*c*) X, a mother, throws a heavy object at her child solely to

frighten him, but the object strikes and kills another child: *R.* v. *Conner* (1835).

7. Actus reus and mens rea. *Actus reus* is the conduct of the accused person and its results; thus, the *actus reus* of homicide is the unlawful killing of Y by X. *Mens rea* is "the guilty mind" or "criminal intention". Almost always, both must be present if a person is to be charged with a crime.

(*a*) The general rule is *actus non facit reum nisi mens sit rea* (an act does not itself constitute guilt unless the mind is guilty). This is a cardinal doctrine of English law. The physical element (the deed) and the mental element are both essential. Hence, if X is to be convicted of theft (*see* XIV, **4**), the prosecution must prove beyond reasonable doubt that X appropriated property belonging to Y, that the appropriation had been carried out by X dishonestly and with the intention of permanently depriving Y of that property: *see* Theft Act 1968, s. 1(1). *See Fowler* v. *Padget* (1798); *Younghusband* v. *Luftig* (1949).

(*b*) Where a statute is silent as to *mens rea*, the presumption that it is required may be rebutted: *see R.* v. *Prince* (1875); *Sherras* v. *de Rutzen* (1895); *Harding* v. *Price* (1948). The term "strict liability" is used in this context.

(*c*) Where X has delegated his authority to his servant Y, X will generally be liable for Y's infringement of a statute concerning the running of a business. *See Allen* v. *Whitehead* (1930); *Barker* v. *Levison* (1951). The term "vicarious responsibility" is used in this context.

8. Parties to a crime. Parties may be known as principals in the first degree (the actual perpetrators of the offence) or principals in the second degree (those who aided and abetted the commission of the offence at the very time it was committed). It is an offence to perform an act with intent to impede the apprehension or prosecution of a person who has committed an arrestable offence: Criminal Law Act 1967, s. 4(1). *See* Magistrates' Courts Act 1980, s. 44; *D.P.P. for N. Ireland* v. *Maxwell* (1978); *R.* v. *Dunnington* (1984)—it is an offence to aid and abet an *attempt* to commit a crime.

GENERAL DEFENCES TO CRIMINAL RESPONSIBILITY

9. Preliminary matters. *See* **6** above. Clearly, there are circumstances in which persons charged with criminal offences may have defences of a general or special nature. The following general defences are mentioned below:

(*a*) mistake (*see* **10** below);

    (*b*) compulsion (*see* **11** below);
    (*c*) intoxication (*see* **12** below);
    (*d*) automatism (*see* **13** below);
    (*e*) insanity (*see* **14** below).
Other variations in liability are considered in **15** below.

10. Mistake. Where X pleads mistake, he is suggesting that the mistake prevented his having the *mens rea* necessary for the offence with which he is being charged; for example, that, on a charge of theft, X had honestly, but mistakenly as it turned out, thought that Y's property which he took, belonged, in fact, to him. A mistake is accepted as a defence only if it is such that, had the facts been as X believed they were, there would have been no *actus reus* (*see R.* v. *Levett* (1638)). The mistake must be reasonable (*see R.* v. *King* (1964)) and it must be a mistake of fact, not of law. Ignorance of the law does not excuse (*see R.* v. *Bailey* (1800); *D.P.P* v. *Morgan* (1976); *R.* v. *Barrett* (1981)).

11. Compulsion. Where A seizes B's hand, places a pistol in it and causes B to shoot C, liability for C's death will not be attributed to B. The following defences based on compulsions are important:

    (*a*) *Duress by threats.* This is seen where X commits an act as the direct consequence of Y's threats. In *D.P.P. for N. Ireland* v. *Lynch* (1975) the House of Lords held that, on a charge of murder, it is open to a person accused as a principal in the second degree (i.e. as an aider and abettor) to plead duress. The threat must be of a serious nature; it will not be accepted if the accused had the opportunity to escape from the threat. *See* also *R.* v. *Graham* (1982).

    (*b*) *Necessity.* This defence may arise where X, faced with committing a wrong or allowing a greater evil to take place, chooses to commit the crime. *See* plea of self-defence under the Criminal Law Act 1967, s. 3(1).

12. Intoxication. Voluntary drunkenness may be a defence where it has produced temporary insanity, or where it negatives the existence of specific *mens rea.* In *D.P.P.* v. *Majewski* (1977) the House of Lords answered affirmatively the question whether a defendant may properly be convicted of assault notwithstanding that, by reason of self-induced intoxication, he did not intend to do the act alleged to contribute to the assault. *See R.* v. *Hardie* (1984).

13. Automatism. This is defined as "an act done by the muscles without any control by the mind, such as a reflex action ... or ... an act done ... while sleepwalking": *per* Lord Denning in *Bratty* v. *A.-G. for N. Ireland* (1963). Where an *actus reus* involves some act on the part of the accused that act must be willed by him. *See R.* v. *Quick and Paddison* (1973); *Moses* v. *Winder* (1981).

14. Insanity. The *M'Naghten Rules* (1843) stated the general position in law regarding insanity. To establish a defence on the ground of insanity, it must be clearly proved that, at the time of committing the act, the party accused was labouring under such a defect of reason, from disease of mind, as not to know the nature and quality of the act he was doing; or if he did know it, that he did not know that what he was doing was wrong. But if the accused was conscious that the act was one which he ought not to do and if that act was at the same time contrary to the law of the land, he is punishable. *See R.* v. *M'Naghten* (1843); *R.* v. *Clarke* (1972); *R.* v. *Sullivan* (1983); *R.* v. *Dickie* (1984).

15. Other variations in liability. Diplomatic immunity may render persons not liable to criminal proceedings. Young persons under ten years are conclusively presumed to be incapable of crime; between ten to fourteen years the presumption may be rebutted by proof that the child knew that what he was doing was wrong; and above fourteen years, persons are presumed fully responsible for their actions.

CONSPIRACY AND ATTEMPT

16. Definition of conspiracy. "If a person agrees with any other person or persons that a course of conduct shall be pursued which will necessarily amount to or involve the commission of any offence or offences by one of the parties to the agreement if the agreement is carried out in accordance with their intentions, he is guilty of conspiracy to commit the offence or offences in question": Criminal Law Act 1977, s. 1(1). A person is not guilty of conspiracy to commit any offence if he is an intended victim of that offence: Criminal Law Act 1977, s. 2(1). It is not an offence to attempt to commit conspiracy: Criminal Law Act 1977, s. 5(7). *See R.* v. *Duncalf* (1979); *R.* v. *Fitzmaurice* (1983); *R.* v. *Ilyas* (1984).

17. Attempt. "If, with intent to commit an offence to which this section applies, a person does an act which is more than merely preparatory to the commission of the offence, he is guilty of attempting to commit the offence": Criminal Attempts Act 1981, s. 1(1). Attempt to commit an offence requires intent: *see R.* v. *Mohan* (1976).

(*a*) Section 1(1) applies to any offence which, if completed, would be triable as an indictable offence, except conspiracy, aiding and abetting, assisting offenders or accepting consideration for not disclosing information about an arrestable offence: s. 1(4).

(*b*) A person may be guilty of attempting to commit an offence even though the facts are such that the commission of the offence is impossible: s.1(2).

PROGRESS TEST 12

1. What is a "crime"? **(2)**
2. What is an "arrestable offence"? **(4)**
3. Define *"actus reus"* and *"mens rea"*. **(7)**
4. What is a "principal in the first degree"? **(8)**
5. When is mistake acceptable as a defence? **(10)**
6. Is duress ever a defence? **(11)**
7. What is meant in law by automatism? **(13)**
8. Outline the essence of the *M'Naghten Rules*. **(14)**
9. Can a child of thirteen be charged with a crime? **(15)**
10. Define conspiracy and attempt. **(16, 17)**

CHAPTER XIII

Criminal Law (2): Offences against the Person

INTRODUCTORY MATTERS

1. Essence of these offences. Offences against the person cover those crimes involving some kind of unlawful violence; they range from murder (which, until twenty years ago, carried the death penalty) to acts such as unlawful wounding.

2. Matters to be covered. The following offences are mentioned below:

   (*a*) murder (*see* **3–6** below);
   (*b*) manslaughter (*see* **7–10** below);
   (*c*) suicide (*see* **11–12** below);
   (*d*) assault and battery (*see* **13–15** below);
   (*e*) unlawful wounding (*see* **16–19** below).

HOMICIDE (1): MURDER

3. Preliminary matters. Homicide is the killing of a human being by a human being. It has been classified as:

   (*a*) *lawful homicide*, e.g. as where death is caused in the execution of the lawful sentence of a competent court (so that there is no *actus reus*) or where death is caused in the advancement of justice (e.g. as in effecting a lawful arrest): *see* Criminal Law Act 1967, s. 3(1);

   (*b*) *unlawful homicide*, e.g. murder (*see* **4** below).

4. Definition of murder. Murder has not been defined by statute. The appropriate definition is that of Coke: "... when any man of sound memory, and of the age of discretion, unlawfully killeth within any county of the realm any reasonable creature *in rerum natura* under the king's peace, with malice aforethought, either expressed by the party or implied by law, so as the party wounded, or hurt, etc., die of the wound or hurt, etc., within a year and a day after the same": Inst. iii, 47.

   (*a*) "*Sound memory and of the age of discretion*". This has been taken to mean one to whom criminal responsibility may be attached.

It excludes, for example, persons under ten years and persons within the *M'Naghten Rules* (*see* XII, **14**).

(*b*) "*Reasonable creature in rerum natura*". This means any human being.

(*c*) "*Malice aforethought*". This is the *mens rea* of murder. It consists of an intention on the part of the accused to kill or cause grievous bodily harm to another person. There exists "no warrant for giving the words 'grievous bodily harm' a meaning other than that which the words convey in their ordinary and natural meaning. 'Bodily harm' needs no explanation and 'grievous' means no more and no less than 'really serious'": *per* Viscount Kilmuir in *D.P.P.* v. *Smith* (1961). *See* also *Hyam* v. *D.P.P.* (1975); *R.* v. *Williamson and Ellerton* (1978).

5. Penalty for murder. The Murder (Abolition of Death Penalty) Act 1965 abolished the offence of capital murder. Under s. 1, a person found guilty of murder must be sentenced to life imprisonment. The court is empowered, under s. 1(2), at the time of sentencing, to recommend a minimum period of imprisonment which is to be served before the convicted person is released on licence.

6. Diminished responsibility and provocation. On a charge of murder, the following may be pleaded:

(*a*) *Diminished responsibility*, under the Homicide Act 1957, s. 2. "(1) Where a person kills or is party to the killing of another, he shall not be convicted of murder if he was suffering from such abnormality of mind (whether arising from a condition of arrested or retarded development of mind or any inherent causes or induced by disease or injury) as substantially impaired his mental responsibility for his acts and omissions in doing or being a party to the killing ... (3) A person who but for this section would be liable, whether as principal or accessory, to be convicted of murder shall be liable instead to be convicted of manslaughter." *See R.* v. *Byrne* (1960); *R.* v. *Dix* (1982); *R.* v. *Chambers* (1983).

(*b*) *Provocation*. "Where on a charge of murder there is evidence on which the jury can find that the person charged was provoked (whether by things done or by things said or by both together) to lose his self-control, the question whether the provocation was enough to make a reasonable man do as he did shall be left to be determined by the jury; and in determining that question the jury shall take into account everything both done and said according to the effect which, in their opinion, it would have on a reasonable man": Homicide Act 1957, s. 3. *See R.* v. *Whitfield* (1976); *D.P.P.* v. *Camplin* (1978); *R.* v. *Raven* (1982).

HOMICIDE (2): MANSLAUGHTER

7. Preliminary matters. Manslaughter has been classified thus:

(a) *voluntary*, as in the case of a killing which would have been murder, but is now considered as manslaughter because, for example, the accused successfully pleads provocation or diminished responsibility (*see* **6** above);

(b) *involuntary*, as in the case of a killing unaccompanied by malice aforethought as where that killing results from an unlawful act likely to cause bodily harm which is not grievous, or from an omission to perform a duty required by the criminal law, or as where the accused has performed an act with criminal negligence.

8. Definition of manslaughter. The offence may be defined as unlawful homicide unaccompanied by malice aforethought.

9. "Unlawful act". *See* **7**(b) above. Where Y's death results from the performance by X of an unlawful act likely to cause bodily harm which is not grievous (i.e. lacking in some element of the *mens rea* necessary for murder) X may be found guilty of manslaughter. It must be an act such as "all sober and reasonable people would inevitably recognise must subject the other person to, at least, the risk of some harm resulting therefrom, albeit not serious harm": *per* Edmund-Davies J. in *R.* v. *Church* (1966). *See R.* v. *Lamb* (1967); *D.P.P.* v. *Newbury and Jones* (1976), *R.* v. *Dalby* (1982); *R.* v. *Mitchell* (1983)—accused argued with and struck A, who fell against B, aged 89—B suffered a broken femur and died, following a subsequent operation, from a pulmonary embolism—accused's appeal against conviction for manslaughter was dismissed.

10. Omission to perform a duty. In some cases a person owes a duty to another and where his failure to perform that duty results in a death, he may be charged with manslaughter. The duty must be one recognised by the criminal law and the breach must have unintentionally resulted in death. *See R.* v. *Instan* (1893); *R.* v. *Bonnyman* (1942); *R.* v. *Stone* (1977).

SUICIDE

11. Present position. Self-slaughter is no longer a crime: Suicide Act 1961, s. 1. But under s. 2 it is an offence to aid, abet, counsel or procure the suicide of another, or an attempt by another to commit suicide. *See R.* v. *McShane* (1977); *R.* v. *Reed* (1982).

12. Suicide pacts. A suicide pact is defined as "a common agreement between two or more persons having for its object the death of all of them, whether or not each is to take his own life, but nothing done by a person who enters into a suicide pact shall be treated as done by him in pursuance of the pact unless it is done while he has the settled intention of dying in pursuance of the pact"; Homicide Act 1957, s. 4(3). If the deceased has killed himself, the survivor of the pact is guilty of the offence under the Suicide Act 1961.

ASSAULT, BATTERY AND UNLAWFUL WOUNDING

13. Preliminary matters. Terms such as "assault" and "battery" have very precise meanings in the criminal law. Although in common usage the terms are often employed synonymously, they have distinct meanings in law, so that a conviction for "assault *or* battery" will be quashed: *see Jones* v. *Sherwood* (1942).

14. Assault. An assault is an act by which any person, intentionally, or, possibly, recklessly, causes another person to fear the immediate application to himself of unlawful physical violence: *see Fagan* v. *Metropolitan Police Commissioner* (1969).

(*a*) The *actus reus* of assault is constituted by the creation in the mind of a person the belief that force is to be used unlawfully against him. The *mens rea* is the intention to create in a person's mind fear of the immediate and unlawful application of physical force. "The *actus reus* of assault is an act which causes another person to apprehend immediate and unlawful violence. The *mens rea* corresponds exactly. The prosecution must prove that the accused foresaw that his act would probably cause another person to have apprehension of immediate and unlawful violence or would possibly have had that consequence, such being the purpose of the act, or that he was reckless as to whether or not his act caused such apprehension. This foresight (the term of art is 'intention') or recklessness is the *mens rea* in assault": *per* Lord Simon in *D.P.P.* v. *Morgan* (1975).

(*b*) There is an assault, therefore, where X points at Y a gun he (X) knows to be unloaded and threatens to shoot him. Y fears that he is to be shot. *See R.* v. *St. George* (1840). There is assault where X advances on Y, shakes his fist angrily and threatens to beat him there and then, so that Y is put in fear of immediate violence. *See R.* v. *Barrett* (1981); *Collins* v. *Willcock* (1984).

15. Battery. This is the actual, intended use of unlawful force on another person without his consent. The *actus reus* is the actual application of unlawful personal violence. Violence includes the slightest force so that no actual harm need result: *see Cole* v. *Turner* (1705). The *mens rea* is constituted by X's intention to apply unlawful personal force against Y. *See R. v. Venna* (1975); *Freeman v. Home Office* (1984).

(*a*) There is battery, therefore, where, for example, X, without lawful excuse, strikes Y's face, or where X, without lawful excuse, intentionally pushes Y off the pavement.

(*b*) Assault and battery are also torts (*see* XVI, **17**).

(*c*) Defences include consent (as where X and Y are boxing), but note that fraud vitiates consent: *see R. v. Clarence* (1888); self-defence (see the Criminal Law Act 1967, s. 3); and lawful and reasonable chastisement (*see Cleary v. Booth* (1893)).

16. Wounding with intent. The essence of this offence is contained within the Offences against the Person Act 1861, s. 18, as amended by the Criminal Law Act 1967, s. 10(2). "Whosoever shall unlawfully and maliciously by any means whatsoever wound or cause any grievous bodily harm to any person ... with intent ... to do some grievous bodily harm to any person, or with intent to resist or prevent the lawful apprehension or detainer of any person ... shall be liable to imprisonment." This offence is commonly known as "wounding with intent". *See R. v. Belfon* (1976).

17. Malicious wounding. The essence of this offence is contained within the Offences against the Person Act 1861, s. 20. "Whosoever shall unlawfully and maliciously wound or inflict any grievous bodily harm upon any other person, either with or without any weapon or instrument ... shall be liable ... to imprisonment." This offence is commonly known as "unlawful" or "malicious wounding". *See R. v. Cunningham* (1957); *Flack v. Hunt* (1979).

18. "Maliciously". "In any statutory definition of a crime, 'malice' must be taken not in the old vague sense of 'wickedness' in general, but as requiring either (1) an actual intention to do the particular kind of harm that was done; or (2) recklessness as to whether such harm would occur or not. ... It is neither limited to, nor does it indeed require, any ill will towards the person injured": Kenny.

19. "Wound", "grievous bodily harm" and "inflict". The term "wound" is used in a very restricted sense and refers to a breaking of the whole skin, so that a scratch or burn is not necessarily a wound. In *R. v. Wood* (1830) the breaking of a collar-bone was held not to constitute wounding since the skin was not breached (*see J.J.C. v. Eisenhower* (1983)). "Grievous bodily harm" means any really serious bodily harm: *see D.P.P. v. Smith* (1961) in **4**(*c*) above. "Inflict" is not confined to direct infliction: *see R. v. Martin* (1881); *R. v. Halliday* (1889), where it was held that grievous bodily harm had been inflicted where X had so frightened Y that Y jumped from a window and sustained injuries. "If a man creates in another man's mind an immediate sense of danger which causes such a person to try to escape, and in so doing he injures himself, the person who creates such a state of mind is responsible for the injuries which result": *per* Lord Coleridge.

PROGRESS TEST 13

1. What is the *mens rea* of murder?   **(4)**
2. Explain "diminished responsibility".   **(6)**
3. Explain the essence of the defence of provocation.   **(6)**
4. Define manslaughter.   **(8)**
5. Explain "omission to perform a duty" in relation to manslaughter.   **(10)**
6. Is suicide a crime?   **(11)**
7. X, without touching Y, creates a reasonable fear in Y's mind that he is about to be struck by X, there and then. Does this constitute assault?   **(14)**
8. What is meant by "battery"?   **(15)**
9. Explain "wounding with intent".   **(16)**
10. What is meant by "grievous bodily harm"?   **(19)**

CHAPTER XIV

Criminal Law (3): Offences Against Property; Other Offences

INTRODUCTORY MATTERS

1. Essence of these offences. Two groups of offences are considered below. First, offences against the property of others; secondly, a group of disparate offences relating to the marriage ceremony, the misuse of controlled drugs and the giving of false evidence.

2. Matters to be covered. The following points are considered below:

    (*a*) theft (*see* **3–6** below);
    (*b*) robbery and burglary (*see* **7** below);
    (*c*) other offences under the Theft Acts 1968, 1978 (*see* **8–11** below);
    (*d*) restitution (*see* **12** below);
    (*e*) criminal damage (*see* **13** below);
    (*f*) forgery and counterfeiting (*see* **14** below);
    (*g*) bigamy (*see* **15–17** below);
    (*h*) misuse of controlled drugs (*see* **18** below);
    (*i*) perjury (*see* **19** below);
    (*j*) contempt (*see* **20** below).

THEFT AND ALLIED OFFENCES

3. Preliminary matters. Prior to 1968, theft, which had been defined in the thirteenth century by Bracton as "the fraudulent handling of another's property without his agreement and with the intention of stealing it", was governed for over half a century by the Larceny Act 1916. This Act gave rise to serious difficulties in interpretation in practice, so that its reform became essential. Reform was achieved by the Theft Act 1968.

4. Definition of theft. "A person is guilty of theft if he dishonestly appropriates property belonging to another with the intention of permanently depriving the other of it; and 'thief' and 'steal' shall be construed accordingly." The *actus reus* of theft is, therefore, the appropriation of another's property; the *mens rea* is dishonesty in appropriation together with the intention of permanently depriving the other person of that property. *See Lawrence* v. *Metropolitan Police Commissioner* (1972); *R.* v. *Harris* (1983).

5. Dishonest appropriation. Generally, a jury requires no direction by a judge as to the meaning of "dishonesty": *R.* v. *Feely* (1973). Under s. 2 of the 1968 Act, a person's appropriation of property belonging to another is not to be regarded as dishonest if he appropriates the property in the belief that he has a right in law to deprive another of it, or in the belief that he would have the other's consent if the other knew of the appropriation and its circumstances, or if he appropriates the property in the belief that the owner cannot be discovered by taking reasonable steps. *See R.* v. *Ghosh* (1982).

6. Intention of permanently depriving. This important concept in the law of theft is dealt with in the following manner by the 1968 Act, s. 6: "A person appropriating property belonging to another without meaning the other permanently to lose the thing itself is nevertheless to be regarded as having the intention of permanently depriving the other of it if his intention is to treat the thing as his own to dispose of regardless of the other's rights; and a borrowing or lending of it may amount to so treating it if, but only if, the borrowing or lending is for a period and in circumstances, making it equivalent to an outright taking or disposal . . ." *See R.* v. *Warner* (1970); *R.* v. *Downes* (1983).

7. Robbery and burglary. At common law, robbery was a capital offence, constituted by the taking of another's goods by violence or by putting that other in fear. Under the 1968 Act, s. 8(1), a person is guilty of *robbery* "if he steals and immediately before or at the time of doing so, and in order to do so, he uses force on any person or puts or seeks to put any person in fear of being then and there subjected to force". A person is guilty of *burglary* under the 1968 Act, s. 9(1), if:

"(*a*) he enters any building or part of a building as a trespasser and with intent to commit any such offence as is mentioned in subsection (2) [i.e. stealing, inflicting grievous bodily harm, raping, doing unlawful damage to the building]; or

(*b*) having entered any building or part of a building as a trespasser he steals or attempts to steal anything in the building or that part of it or inflicts or attempts to inflict on any person therein any grievous bodily harm." *See R.* v. *Dawson* (1978); *R.* v. *Gregory* (1982).

8. Handling stolen property. "A person handles stolen goods if (otherwise than in the course of the stealing) knowing or believing them to be stolen goods he dishonestly receives the goods, or dishonestly undertakes or assists in their retention, removal, disposal or realisation by or for the benefit of another person, or if he arranges to do so": 1968 Act, s. 22(1). *See R.* v. *Pethick* (1980); *R.* v. *Bloxham* (1982); *Broom* v. *Crowther* (1984).

9. Obtaining property by deception. "A person who by any deception dishonestly obtains property belonging to another, with the intention of permanently depriving the other of it, shall on conviction be liable to imprisonment ...": 1968 Act, s. 15(1). There is an offence under s. 15, therefore, where X obtains money from Y by promising to mow Y's lawn and where X fails to do so, having had no intention whatsoever of doing that work. *See R.* v. *Gilmartin* (1983).

10. Obtaining a pecuniary advantage by deception. "A person who by any deception dishonestly obtains for himself or another any pecuniary advantage shall ... be liable to imprisonment": 1968 Act, s. 16(1). There is an offence under s. 16, therefore, where X stays at a hotel for a night, intending to leave soon after dawn without paying for his accommodation, and he leaves without paying. *See* also Theft Act 1978 (repealing Theft Act 1968, s. 16(2)(*a*)): "A person who by any deception dishonestly obtains services from another shall be guilty of an offence": s. 1(1). It is an offence under s. 3(1) to "make off", dishonestly, without paying for goods or services supplied: *see R.* v. *McDavitt* (1981); *R.* v. *Brooks* (1983).

NOTE: "Deception" means "any deception (whether deliberate or reckless) by words or conduct as to fact or as to law, including a deception as to the present intentions of the person using the deception or any other person": 1968 Act, s. 15(4).

11. Blackmail. Under the 1968 Act, s. 21(1): "A person is guilty of blackmail, if, with a view to gain for himself or another or with intent to cause loss to another, he makes any unwarranted demand with menaces; and for this purpose a demand with menaces is unwarranted unless the person making it does so in the belief:

(*a*) that he had reasonable grounds for making the demand; *and*

(*b*) that the use of menaces is a proper means of reinforcing the demand." *See Treacy* v. *D.P.P.* (1971); *R.* v. *Harvey* (1981); *R.* v. *Cutbill* (1982).

12. Orders for restitution. Where goods have been stolen and a person is convicted of any offence in connection with the theft, the court may order anyone having possession or control of the goods to restore them to any person entitled to recover them from him: *see* 1968 Act, s. 28(1)(*a*). *See R.* v. *Pope* (1978); *R.* v. *Thibeault* (1983).

13. Criminal damage. Under the Criminal Damage Act 1971, it is an offence, intentionally or recklessly and without lawful excuse to destroy or damage another's property.

(*a*) "Recklessly" encompasses a failure to give any thought as to whether there was any risk where, if any thought were given to the matter, it would be obvious that there was: *R.* v. *Caldwell* (1982).

(*b*) *See R.* v. *Denton* (1981); *R.* v. *Miller* (1983).

14. Forgery and counterfeiting. "A person is guilty of forgery if he makes a false instrument with the intention that he or another shall use it to induce somebody to accept it as genuine, and by reason of so accepting it to do or not to do some act to his own or any person's prejudice": Forgery and Counterfeiting Act 1981, s. 1. Under the 1981 Act, s. 14: "(1) It is an offence for a person to make a counterfeit of a currency note or of a protected coin, intending that he or another shall pass or tender it as genuine. (2) It is an offence for a person to make a counterfeit of a currency note or of a protected coin without lawful authority or excuse." (A "protected coin" is one which is customarily used as money in any country, or is specified as such in a Treasury order.) *See R.* v. *Donnelly* (1984); *R.* v. *Campbell* (1984).

OTHER OFFENCES: BIGAMY, MISUSE OF DRUGS, PERJURY AND CONTEMPT

15. Bigamy. "Whosoever being married, shall marry any other person during the life of the former husband or wife, whether the second marriage shall have taken place in England or Ireland or elsewhere" is guilty of an offence: Offences against the Person Act 1861, s. 57. Example: X marries Y. Two years later, in full knowledge that his marriage to Y, who is alive, is valid, he goes through a ceremony of marriage with Z. *See R.* v. *Allen* (1872).

16. Proof of the offence. To prove bigamy, it is necessary for the prosecution to show: proof of the first marriage of the accused, its validity, and its subsistence at the date of the second ceremony; proof of a second ceremony of marriage by the accused with some person other than the lawful spouse.

17. Defences. The accused may prove, for example, that his former marriage was null and void. Other defences include: continuous absence by the spouse for seven years in circumstances in which the spouse was not known to have been living during that time; dissolution of the first marriage; honest belief that the prior marriage was void or had been dissolved; belief in death of spouse. *See R.* v. *Tolson* (1889); *R.* v. *Taylor* (1950); *R.* v. *Gould* (1968).

18. Misuse of drugs. The grave problem of drug dependence has led to legislation designed to control the misuse of certain types of drugs, known, under the Misuse of Drugs Act 1971, as "controlled drugs". They include: Class A drugs (cocaine, heroin, opium, etc.); Class B drugs (amphetamine, cannabis, etc.); Class C drugs (pemoline, etc.). Classification affects the maximum penalties for some offences under the Act. *See R. v. Champ* (1982); *R. v. Aramah* (1983).

(*a*) Under the 1971 Act it is an offence to have a controlled drug in one's possession (except under licence), to knowingly permit the use of drugs on one's premises, to supply or attempt to supply such drugs, etc. *See R. v. King* (1978); *Taylor v. Chief Constable of Kent* (1981); *R. v. Taafe* (1984).

(*b*) It is a defence, under s. 28, to show that the accused took possession of the drug for the purpose of preventing another from committing an offence if the accused proves that he neither believed nor suspected nor had reason to suspect that the substance or product in question was a controlled drug. *See Warner v. Metropolitan Police Commissioner* (1969); *Sweet v. Parsley* (1970).

19. Perjury. "If any person lawfully sworn as a witness or as an interpreter in a judicial proceeding wilfully makes a statement material in that proceeding, which he knows to be false or does not believe to be true, he shall be guilty of perjury"; Perjury Act 1911, s. 1(1).

(*a*) *Examples of perjury.* At the trial of Y, X, lawfully sworn as a witness, is giving evidence on the material question of whether Y was in Portsmouth or Plymouth on a certain day. X will be guilty of perjury if he states that Y was in Portsmouth, knowing, in fact, that this was not so; or if he states that Y was in Plymouth, which, in fact, was true, but believing his statement to be untrue; or if he states that Y was in Plymouth, which, in fact, was true, but he is reckless as to whether his statement is true or not. *See R. v. Hall* (1982).

(*b*) *Subornation of perjury.* "Every person who aids, abets, counsels, procures or suborns another person to commit an offence against this Act shall be liable to be proceeded against, indicted, tried and punished as if he were a principal offender": s. 7. *See R. v. Cromack* (1978).

(*c*) *Corroboration.* The falsity of a statement must be proved either by two witnesses or by one witness who is corroborated by proof of other material, relevant facts: *see R. v. Yates* (1841); *R. v. O'Connor* (1980).

20. Contempt of court. Criminal contempt includes contempt in the face of the court (e.g. words or actions in court which interfere with the course of justice: *see Morris v. Master of the Crown Office* (1970)—

interruption of proceedings by chanting slogans); conduct which scandalises the court (e.g. publication of scurrilous abuse of a judge in his judicial capacity: see *A.-G.* v. *B.B.C.* (1981)); conduct interfering with or obstructing the due process of the court (e.g. publication of names of witnesses in defiance of judge's instructions: *see R.* v. *Socialist Worker Printers* (1975)).

(*a*) Under the Contempt of Court Act 1981, the "strict liability rule", whereby conduct may be treated as a contempt as tending to interfere with the course of justice, regardless of intent to do so, applies only to publications addressed to the public or any section of it, which create a substantial risk that the course of justice in the proceedings in question will be "seriously impeded or prejudiced": s. 2.

(*b*) *See A.-G.* v. *English* (1982); *Home Office* v. *Harman* (1982); *Secretary of State for Defence* v. *Guardian Newspapers* (1984).

PROGRESS TEST 14

1. What is meant by "theft" under the Theft Act 1968?   **(4)**
2. Explain "dishonest appropriation".   **(5)**
3. Define robbery.   **(7)**
4. In what circumstances does a person "handle" stolen goods? **(8)**
5. What is blackmail?   **(11)**
6. When is the offence of forgery committed?   **(14)**
7. In what circumstances is the offence of bigamy committed? **(15)**
8. Are there any defences to a charge of bigamy?   **(17)**
9. Outline some of the offences relating to controlled drugs.   **(18)**
10. What is perjury?   **(19)**
11. What is contempt of court?   **(20)**

CHAPTER XV

Civil Law (I): Contract

INTRODUCTORY MATTERS

1. Essence of contract. Where persons exhange the fruits of their labour through the medium of money—as is common in our society—agreement is essential, and the enforcement of agreement becomes a necessity if an organised system of commerce is to exist and thrive. The essence of contract is *agreement* between parties.

2. Definition of contract. Not every agreement is a contract. Thus, there would be no contract if two friends promise to meet each other for lunch on a certain day, or where a person enters a football pool competition based on a clause stating that the competition is based on an agreement "binding in honour only": *see Jones* v. *Vernons Pools* (1938). A contract is an *agreement* between two or more persons which is *intended* by them *to have legal consequences*. It is essentially an agreement which binds the parties, so that it will be upheld by the courts.

3. Classification of contracts. Contracts may be classified as follows:

(*a*) *Simple contracts.* These derive their force from mutual agreement. They require the essentials mentioned in **4** below.

(*b*) *Specialty contracts*, e.g. deeds. These derive their force from the very form in whch they are recorded.

(*c*) *Contracts of record.* There are obligations deriving their force from the authority of the courts, e.g. judgments, recognisances.

4. Essentials of a contract. A simple contract requires the following:

(*a*) an intention to create legal relations (*see* **6** below);

(*b*) offer and acceptance (*see* **7–8** below);

(*c*) contractual capacity of the parties (*see* **9** below);

(*d*) valuable consideration (*see* **10–11** below);

(*e*) legality of object (*see* **14** below);

(*f*) genuineness of consent (*see* **15** below);

(*g*) possibility of performance (an agreement obviously impossible of performance will not be upheld);

(*h*) certainty of terms (the terms of a contract should be, as far as possible, certain).

INTENTION, OFFER AND ACCEPTANCE AND CONTRACTUAL CAPACITY

5. Preliminaries. The parties must intend that the agreement shall result in legal consequences. Further, there must be an offer, express or implied, which is accepted in express or implied fashion. Additionally, the parties must have full capacity to contract; thus, if one party should lack, for example, the mental capacity to understand a contract, the agreement may not be upheld. These vital matters are discussed in this section.

6. Intention to create legal relations. Where parties do not intend to be bound, there is, in general, no contract. Where a clause excludes the jurisdiction of the court, there is generally no contract: *see Rose, Frank & Co.* v. *Crompton Bros.* (1923). A mere "domestic agreement" will generally be held not contractual: *see Balfour* v. *Balfour* (1919). *See* also *Pettitt* v. *Pettitt* (1970).

7. Offer. An offer—which is essential to any contract—may be made orally or in writing, or it may be implied from conduct.

(*a*) An offer may be made to a specific person (in which case he alone may accept) or to a specific group (any of whom may accept) or to the world at large (when anyone may accept). Thus, in *Carlill* v. *Carbolic Smoke Ball Co. Ltd.* (1893), X bought an influenza preventive from a firm which had advertised to pay £100 to any person contracting influenza during a stated period after using the preventive. X contracted influenza and sued the company successfully. It was held that the company's offer had been accepted by X.

(*b*) The offer must be firm, i.e. it must be more than a mere "invitation to treat" (as where goods are on display in a shop): *see Pharmaceutical Society of Great Britain* v. *Boots* (1953); *C. A. Norgren Co.* v. *Technomarketing* (1983)—pricelist sent to potential customer is merely an invitation to treat.

(*c*) An offer will lapse: if the offeree dies before acceptance; if the offer is not accepted within the stated time or a reasonable time (*see Ramsgate Victoria Hotel* v. *Montefiore* (1866)); if the offeree does not make a valid acceptance; or if he makes a mere counter-offer.

(*d*) An offer may be revoked any time before acceptance. Revocation must be communicated before acceptance: *see Dickinson* v. *Dodds* (1876).

8. Acceptance. An acceptance may be oral, in writing or implied from the conduct of the parties. *See* Sale of Goods Act 1979, s. 35.

(*a*) Acceptance must be absolute and unqualified. Once made, it cannot be revoked. *See Hyde* v. *Wrench* (1840).

(*b*) A mere enquiry is not a counter-offer: *Stevenson* v. *McLean* (1880).

(*c*) The offeree's acceptance must be positive, so that it will not be implied from silence alone. *See Felthouse* v. *Bindley* (1862).

(*d*) The acceptance must reach the offeror (or his agent). *See Entores* v. *Miles Far East Co.* (1955).

9. Capacity to make a contract. Persons in certain categories may lack contractual capacity.

(*a*) *Drunken persons*, who, at the time of contracting, were not aware of the quality of their acts, may avoid the contract, if the other party was aware of this.

(*b*) *Corporations.* Generally, a corporation's acts relating to contracts must be authorised, by the memorandum of association. If a corporation acts otherwise it is said to be acting *ultra vires*—beyond its powers: *see Ashbury Rail Carriage Co.* v. *Riche* (1875); *Re Beauforte Ltd.* (1953). Under the European Communities Act 1972, s. 9(1): "In favour of a person dealing with a company in good faith, any transaction decided on by the directors shall be deemed to be one which is within the capacity of the company to enter into."

(*c*) *Minors* (i.e. persons under eighteen, known also as "infants"). Minors' contracts may be *valid* if they involve necessary goods (or services) suitable to the condition of life of the minor and to his actual requirements at the time of sale and delivery (*see Nash* v. *Inman* (1908)—eleven fancy waistcoats were held not to be necessaries for a minor, who was adequately supplied at the time of the contract). A contract of employment for the minor's benefit as a whole is also binding. Some contracts may be *voidable*, i.e. the minor may repudiate them before his majority or within a reasonable time thereafter. Examples: agreements for the sale of land; agreements to take shares; marriage settlements. *See Steinberg* v. *Scala (Leeds) Ltd.* (1923). They may be *void* if, for example, they relate to money lent to the minor, or if they relate to non-necessaries: Infants' Relief Act 1874.

(*d*) *Mentally disordered persons.* In general, such persons who were incapable of understanding the nature of the contract they entered into, may avoid the contract if the other party was aware of that liability.

THE CONCEPT OF CONSIDERATION

10. Preliminaries. Consideration is that which is given or accepted in return for a promise. It was defined in *Currie* v. *Misa* (1875), thus: "Some right, interest, profit, or benefit accruing to the one party or some forebearance, detriment, loss or responsibility given, suffered or undertaken by another." Example: A buys a book from B for £5.

Here both A and B have provided consideration—A, the money; B, the book. Consideration may be *executory* (as where it consists of a promise to perform an act in the future, e.g. to deliver merchandise); *executed* (as where the act which constitutes the consideration is wholly performed, e.g. where payment is made for goods delivered, say, a week before delivery).

11. Rules relating to consideration. The following rules should be noted:

(*a*) Consideration must be *legal*. Thus, payment made in relation to an agreement to commit a crime is not a valid consideration (*see* **14** below);

(*b*) Consideration must generally *move from the promisee*. One who is seeking to enforce a simple contract must establish that consideration was given by him in return for the very promise he wishes to enforce. *See Tweddle* v. *Atkinson* (1861).

(*c*) Consideration must be *real*, but need not be adequate. *See Thomas* v. *Thomas* (1842)—£1 per year rent was held to be valuable consideration.

(*d*) Consideration must *not be past*. Thus, in *Re McArdle* (1951), X completed repairs to property she shared with her husband, Y, and his mother, Z. On Z's death, the property was sold, the proceeds of the sale being shared among the children of the marriage who signed a document in which they promised to pay for the repairs made by X. It was held that the promise could not be enforced since, when the agreement was made, the consideration was past.

NOTE: In general, consideration is necessary to the validity of every contract not under seal.

VOID AND VOIDABLE CONTRACTS

12. Preliminary matters. A *void* contract is entirely destitute of any legal effect; under no circumstances will it be upheld by the courts. A *voidable* contract is capable of being set aside; it has legal effect until avoided.

13. Contracts void by statute. Some contracts may be void, as a result of statute, unless reduced to writing, e.g. bills of exchange (*see* Bills of Exchange Act 1882). Some may be void unless made by deed, e.g. contracts relating to transfer of land (*see* Law of Property Act 1925). Others may be void under, e.g., the Restrictive Trade Practices Act 1976, s. 35(1).

14. Illegal contracts. Contracts to commit torts or crimes are void. Contracts which may damage the public safety, which damage the administration of justice, or which tend to promote corruption or sexual immorality are also void. *See Pearce* v. *Brooks* (1866); *Re Davstone Estate Ltd.* (1969).

15. Voidable contracts (1). Contracts which may be set aside by the courts at the request of either party are "voidable". They include the following, for example:

(*a*) Contracts entered into as the result of duress, e.g. threatened violence. *See Kaufman* v. *Gerson* (1904)—agreement by X after Y had promised not to prosecute X's husband. *See* also *Pao On* v. *Lau Yiu Long* (1980).

(*b*) Contracts entered into, following undue influence, resulting in the weakening of a party's judgment and exercise of free will. The presumption of undue influence (e.g. in the case of solicitor and client, parent and child) may be disproved by the stronger party showing that the other had received independent legal advice, that the consideration was reasonable and that all material facts had been disclosed. *See Allcard* v. *Skinner* (1877); *National Westminster Bank* v. *Morgan* (1983).

16. Voidable contracts (2). Further examples of voidable contracts are those based on a misrepresentation made by one party to another during negotiations before the contract was made.

(*a*) A misrepresentation is an untrue statement of fact made so as to induce the person to whom it was made to enter the contract.

(*b*) Innocent misrepresentation is an untrue statement of fact which the maker of the statement does believe to be true. Remedies are rescission (i.e. repudiation or termination of the contract) or damages.

(*c*) Negligent misrepresentation (*see* Misrepresentation Act 1967) is an untrue statement of fact which the maker of the statement had reasonable grounds for believing to be true and did, in fact, believe to be true up to the time of making the contract. Remedies are rescission and damages.

(*d*) Fraudulent misrepresentation consists of "an untrue statement made knowingly or without belief in its truth, or recklessly, careless whether it be true or false": *Derry* v. *Peek* (1889). Remedies are rescission and damages (in respect of the tort of deceit).

NOTE: The full disclosure of facts is required in contracts *uberrimae fidei* ("of the utmost good faith"), e.g. contracts of insurance, company prospectuses, contracts for the sale of land.

MISTAKE IN CONTRACT

17. Preliminary matters. Where there is mistake in a contract, there is no *consensus ad idem*, i.e. there is no genuineness of consent. In such cases the agreement may be negatived.

18. Mistake. Where a party to a contract enters the agreement under a mistake, he can avoid the contract if the mistake is one of fact (not of law) *and* the mistake is so fundamental as to negative the agreement. The validity of the contract is not generally affected where a party has made a mistake in the expression of his intention or a mistake or error of judgment.

(*a*) The contract is avoided if there is a mistake as to the nature of the document; if there is a mistake as to the identity of the party contracted with; if there is a common mistake as to the existence of the thing contracted for; if the mistake of one party is known to the other; if there is a mutual mistake as to the identity of the thing contracted for; if there is a common mistake as to the fundamental subject-matter of the agreement.

(*b*) These matters are illustrated in the following cases: *Couturier* v. *Hastie* (1852); *Webster* v. *Cecil* (1861); *Raffles* v. *Wichelhaus* (1864); *Cundy* v. *Lindsay* (1878); *Lewis* v. *Averay* (1972).

19. Rectification. Where it can be shown that the parties had agreed on the terms of the contract, but had written them down incorrectly, the court can order rectification of the instrument recording the agreement. *See Craddock Bros.* v. *Hunt* (1923); *Bates Ltd.* v. *Wyndhams Ltd.* (1981).

DISCHARGE OF CONTRACT AND REMEDIES FOR BREACH

20. Preliminary matters. A contract may be discharged in a variety of ways: *see* **21–22** below. Where discharge is the result of breach, i.e. where the contract is broken, several types of remedies are available to the injured party: *see* **23–24** below.

21. Mode of discharge (1). A contract may be discharged in the following ways, for example:

(*a*) *By performance*. Performance must be complete. If there is part performance only, payment can be enforced for that part where the contract can be divided: *see Hoenig* v. *Isaacs* (1952).

(*b*) *By agreement*. One party may agree that the other shall be released from all his contractual obligations.

(*c*) *By frustration of the agreement*. Discharge by frustration occurs where there has been a change in the law after the agreement has been made, rendering performance impossible (*see Baily* v. *De Crespigny* (1869)); where the subject-matter is destroyed (*see Taylor* v. *Caldwell* (1863)); where personal incapacity prevents performance (see *Robinson* v. *Davison* (1871)); where the contract depends on the occurrence of some event which is cancelled (see *Krell* v. *Henry* (1903)). Under the Law Reform (Frustrated Contracts) Act 1943, where a contract is discharged by frustration, all sums paid before discharge are recoverable, and all sums payable under the contract cease to be payable. See *B.P. Exploration Co.* v. *Hunt* (*No. 2*) (1982).

22. Mode of discharge (2). A contract may be discharged by breach.

(a) In the case of a *breach of condition*, a term "going to the very root of the contract" has been broken, so that the other party can treat the contract as having ended or he can treat it as binding and may sue for damages.

(b) In the case of a *breach of warranty*, an unessential term has been breached, so that the other party may sue for damages.

(c) In the case of *anticipatory breach*, one party repudiates before performance. The other party may sue at once, or await full performance. See *Avery* v. *Bowden* (1856).

23. Remedies for breach (1). The following remedies for breach are available to the injured party:

(a) *Action on quantum meruit* ("what it is worth"). The plaintiff may be awarded what the court decides his work or services are worth. See *Craven-Ellis* v. *Canons Ltd.* (1936).

(b) *Specific performance.* This is an order made by the court instructing the defendant to carry out the agreement. It is not generally granted in the case of an agreement for personal services or where it would cause the defendant undue hardship.

(c) *Injunction.* The court may order a person to perform, or refrain from performing, some act, for example where the act, or non-performance, might cause breach of contract. See *Warner Bros.* v. *Nelson* (1936).

(d) *Rescission.* Where the court is satisfied that both parties can be returned to their pre-contractual positions, the contract may be rescinded.

24. Remedies for breach (2). Damages are an important remedy for breach of contract. The general aim of damages is to put the plaintiff in the same position as if the contract had been carried out fully. See *Hadley* v. *Baxendale* (1854); *Victoria Laundry* v. *Newman Industries Ltd.* (1949); *Jobling* v. *Associated Dairies* (1981).

(a) *Liquidated damages.* These represent the amount agreed upon beforehand by the parties as payable in the event of a breach of contract. They must represent a genuine estimate; they must not be in the nature of a "penalty". See *Ford Motor Co.* v. *Armstrong* (1915).

(*b*) *Unliquidated damages*. These are decided by the court. They may take the following forms:

(*i*) *ordinary damages*: these represent compensation for loss actually suffered by the plaintiff and are considered as arising naturally from the breach;

(*ii*) *special damages*: these represent losses not arising naturally from the breach; generally, they should have been within the parties' contemplation;

(*iii*) *exemplary damages*: these are rarely awarded for breach of contract; they are in excess of a normal award of damages;

(*iv*) *nominal damages*: these are awarded where the plaintiff proves a breach, but where he has suffered no real loss;

(*v*) *contemptuous damages*: these are very small and are awarded where the plaintiff succeeds in his action, but the court wishes to express disapproval of his behaviour.

PROGRESS TEST 15

1. What is a contract? **(2)**
2. Enumerate the essentials of a simple contract. **(4)**
3. What are the general rules relating to offer? **(7)**
4. Can acceptance be implied from conduct only? **(8)**
5. When are minors' contracts valid? **(9)**
6. Define "consideration". **(10)**
7. What is meant by "executed consideration"? **(10)**
8. "Consideration must not be past." Explain. **(11)**
9. What is meant by a voidable contract? **(12)**
10. Explain "innocent misrepresentation". **(16)**
11. What is fraudulent misrepresentation? **(16)**
12. When does mistake allow a party to avoid a contract? **(18)**
13. In what ways may a contract be discharged? **(21, 22)**
14. Explain "*quantum meruit*", "specific performance". **(23)**
15. When are nominal damages awarded? **(24)**
16. What is the general aim of awarding damages? **(24)**

CHAPTER XVI

Civil Law (2): Torts

INTRODUCTORY MATTERS

1. The essence of tort. The word "tort" means "wrong". The law of torts is concerned with the determination of disputes which arise where one person alleges wrong conduct against another. It should be noted that some torts, e.g. assault and battery (*see* **17** below) are torts *and* crimes. Winfield describes liability in tort as arising "from the breach of a duty primarily fixed by the law: this duty is towards persons generally and its breach is redressable by an action for unliquidated damages". This differs from liability in contract, which arises from agreement of the parties; further, it is based on a duty, not to specific persons (as in contract) but to persons generally.

2. The concept of vicarious liability. In some cases X may be responsible in law for the tort of Y; this is an example of vicarious responsibility. Example: X is generally vicariously responsible for the tort of his servant, Y, committed during the course of Y's employment in X's service. *See Limpus* v. *London General Omnibus Co.* (1862); *Lloyd* v. *Grace, Smith & Co.* (1912); *Kooragang Investments* v. *Richardson & Wrench Ltd.* (1982).

3. Classification of torts. One generally adopted scheme is as follows:

    (*a*) wrongs to the person, e.g. assault, battery, false imprisonment;

    (*b*) wrongs to reputation, e.g. defamation;

    (*c*) wrongs to property, e.g. trespass to land;

    (*d*) wrongs to persons or property, e.g. negligence, nuisance.

4. General defences. The following general defences may be pleaded in an action based on tort:

    (*a*) Mistake. *See Hollins* v. *Fowler* (1875).

    (*b*) Statutory authority, as where an Act of Parliament authorises an action which interferes with some person's right. *See A.-G.* v. *Nottingham Corporation* (1904).

    (*c*) Necessity, as where a house on fire is demolished so as to prevent its collapsing into a public highway: *Dewey* v. *White* (1827).

    (*d*) Private defence, as where force is used and harm is caused in a reasonable effort to protect one's property: *see Lowery* v. *Walker* (1911); *Barnard* v. *Evans* (1925).

(*e*) Inevitable accident (i.e. an accident "not avoidable by any such precautions as a reasonable man, doing such an act there and then, could be expected to take": Pollock). *See Stanley* v. *Powell* (1891); *Jones* v. *L.C.C.* (1932).

(*f*) *Volenti non fit injuria* ("that to which a person consents cannot be considered an injury"). Where harm is suffered by the plaintiff with his freely-given assent, this may be a defence. Knowledge is merely evidence of assent: *Dann* v. *Hamilton* (1939). A person does not assent merely because he has knowledge of a potential danger: *Barker* v. *James* (1921). "Knowledge of the risk of injury is not enough. Nor is a willingness to take the risk of injury. Nothing will suffice short of an agreement to waive any claim for negligence": *Nettleship* v. *Weston* (1971).

5. Remedies. These include: abatement (i.e. removal) of a nuisance; action for injunction; damages. Damages may be: contemptuous, as where the court feels that the plaintiff's conduct was such that he may have deserved what was done to him; nominal, as where there is no moral fault on the plaintiff's part; ordinary or substantial (these are the usual type of damages, intended to represent adequate compensation for injury suffered); exemplary (awarded "to teach a wrongdoer that tort does not pay"). *See Rookes* v. *Barnard* (1964); *Drane* v. *Evangelou* (1978).

NEGLIGENCE

6. Preliminary matters. The term "negligence" is used in law to mean a mental attitude of carelessness towards the nature and consequences of one's conduct *or* to refer to a tort arising where there is a breach of a legal duty. It is used below in the latter sense.

7. Definition and essence of negligence. Negligence is the breach of a legal duty to take care, resulting in damage, which was undesired by the defendant, sustained by the plaintiff. The burden of proof (*see* X, 11) is generally on the plaintiff.

(*a*) Whether or not there is a duty to take care was considered in *Donoghue* v. *Stevenson* (1932), in which a retailer sold to X's friend ginger beer in a bottle which contained the remains of a snail. X suffered shock and gastric illness after drinking from the bottle and sued the manufacturer for negligence. The question was whether the facts constituted a cause of action in negligence. "You must take reasonable care to avoid acts or omissions which you can reasonably foresee would be likely to injure your neighbour. Who, then, in law, is my neighbour? The answer seems to be—persons who are so closely and directly affected by my act that I ought reasonably to have them in contemplation as being so affected when I am directing my mind to the acts or omissions which are called in question": *per* Lord Atkin.

(*b*) Negligence "properly connotes the complex concept of duty, breach and damage thereby suffered by the person to whom the duty was owing": *per* Lord Wright in *Lochgelly Iron & Coal Co.* v. *M'Mullan* (1934).

8. What must be proved. If it is to be shown that the defendant was guilty of negligence it must be proved: that there had existed a duty of care (*see* 7(*a*) above) towards the plaintiff; that the defendant had breached the duty by acting in a manner in which a reasonable person would not have acted in those circumstances; that the plaintiff had sustained damage.

9. Res ipsa loquitur ("the thing speaks for itself"). In some cases the mere fact of an accident occurring raises an inference of the defendant's negligence. "You may presume negligence from the mere fact that it happens": *Ballard* v. *N. British Railway* (1923). *See Byrne* v. *Boadle* (1863)—barrel falling from upper floor; *Mahon* v. *Osborne* (1933)—swab left in patient's body; *Ward* v. *Tesco* (1976)—shopper slipping on supermarket floor.

NOTE: "Contributory negligence" (i.e. a man's carelessness in looking after himself) may be a defence where it can be proved that an injured party failed to take reasonable care of himself, thus contributing to his own injury: *Nance* v. *British Columbia Electric Railway* (1951). Under the Law Reform (Contributory Negligence) Act 1945, a claim in respect of damage is reduced to the extent considered by the court as just and equitable, having regard to the claimant's share in responsibility for the damage. *See Harrison* v. *British Railways* (1981).

NUISANCE

10. Preliminary matters. Assume that X acts unlawfully, so that, as a result, Y's property is interfered with, or Y's personal comfort is reduced. X may be held liable following an action for nuisance brought by Y. Y's remedies will include abatement; injunction; action for damages. *See Coventry C.C.* v. *Doyle* (1981).

11. Definition and essence of nuisance. Nuisance may be defined as an unlawful interference with another's use or enjoyment of, or right over, or in relation to, land, or damage resulting from such interference: *see Read* v. *Lyons & Co. Ltd.* (1947). "It is impossible to give any precise or universal formula, but it may broadly be said that a useful test is perhaps what is reasonable according to the ordinary usages of mankind living in society": *Sedleigh-Denfield* v. *O'Callaghan* (1940).

12. Public nuisance. This is nuisance affecting the public "so that annoyance is caused to Her Majesty's subjects". It may also be a crime, e.g. the obstruction of a highway.

13. Private nuisance. This is a nuisance which injures a private person, e.g. by causing unreasonable personal discomfort to him. *See Laws* v. *Florinplace Ltd.* (1981).

TRESPASS

14. Preliminary matters. Any unjustifiable interference with another's rights may be a tort. Thus, "every invasion of private property, be it ever so minute, is a trespass": *Entick* v. *Carrington* (1765). (In some cases trespass may be a crime; thus, trespassing on the premises of a foreign mission may be a crime under the Criminal Law Act 1977, s. 9.)

15. Definition and essence of trespass. Trespass may be defined as an unjustifiable interference by one person with another's rights. Where X acts so that Y's rights are diminished, as where X walks across Y's land without Y's permission, X has committed the tort of trespass. Trespass generally necessitates a direct, rather than a consequential, injury to another's rights. *See R.* v. *Jones* (1976).

16. Trespass to land. Where X acts so that he interferes unjustifiably, directly and immediately with Y's possession of land, X has committed the tort of trespass to land.

(*a*) Such trespass may be actionable *per se*, that is, Y need not prove special damage.

(*b*) X's act may consist in trespass by wrongful entry or by remaining on Y's land, or by placing things on that land. *See Simpson* v. *Weber* (1925).

(*c*) For purposes of the Theft Act 1968, s. 9(1)(*b*), a person is a trespasser if he enters the premises of another knowing that he is entering in excess of the permission given him or being reckless whether he is so doing. *See R.* v. *Jones* (1976).

(*d*) Defences may include: possession of a licence; justification by law.

(*e*) Remedies may include: re-entry; action for ejectment of the trespasser.

17. Trespass to the person. Where X, for example, applies unlawful force to Y, the tort of battery may be committed. Assault and battery (*see* XIII, **14–15**) are common examples of trespass to the person. False imprisonment (i.e. restraining a person's freedom without lawful justification) is another example. Defences include: consent; self-defence; defendant acting to prevent a trespass; defendant acting under the criminal law; defendant exercising parental authority; inevitable accident; statutory authority.

18. Trespass to goods. This tort involves a wrongful interference with possession of goods. The harm done must be direct, e.g. as where X unjustly detains Y's goods. *See* Torts (Interference with Goods) Act 1977; *Hillesden Securities* v. *Ryjack* (1983).

THE RULE IN RYLANDS *v.* FLETCHER

19. Statement of the rule. "We think that the true rule of law is, that the person who, for his own purposes, brings on his land and collects and keeps there anything likely to do mischief if it escapes, must keep it in at his peril; and if he does not do so, is *prima facie* answerable for all the damage which is the natural consequence of its escape. He can excuse himself by showing that the escape was owing to the plaintiff's default; or perhaps that the escape was the consequence of a vis major [irresistible force], or the act of God": *per* Blackburn J. in *Rylands* v. *Fletcher* (1868).

20. The rule in practice. In *Rylands* v. *Fletcher* (1868), the defendants had constructed a reservoir on their land so as to supply water to their mill. On the site of the reservoir was a closed shaft of an old mine, the passage of which led to the plaintiff's adjoining mine. As a result of the engineers' negligence this was not discovered, so that water from the reservoir flooded the plaintiff's mine. The House of Lords held the defendants liable.

21. The rule extended. The rule has been extended to include the escape of gas, poisonous vegetation, etc. *See Crowhurst* v. *Amersham Burial Board* (1878). Essentially, however, there must be an escape of the substance from the defendant's land: *Read* v. *Lyons & Co.* (1947). (But the escape must not be due to the act of a stranger: *Rickards* v. *Lothian* (1913).)

22. Exceptions to the rule. The following exceptions should be noted:

(*a*) The damage must be due to the natural user of the land.

(*b*) The rule does not apply to the land itself, only to things brought and kept on it. *See Davey* v. *Harrow Corporation* (1957).

(*c*) The rule will not apply where the plaintiff has consented to the bringing or keeping of the things in question on the defendant's land. *See A.-G.* v. *Cory Bros.* (1921).

(*d*) The rule does not apply to damage caused by an act of God: *Nichols* v. *Marsland* (1876)—unusually violent storm resulting in collapse of bridges.

DEFAMATION

23. Preliminary matters. The making of false statements about a man to his general discredit is usually a tort, in that it is an unjustifiable interference with the right in every man "to have the estimation in which he stands in the opinion of others unaffected by false statements to his discredit": *per* Cave J. in *Scott* v. *Sampson* (1882). *See Youssoupoff* v. *M.G.M. Ltd.* (1934).

24. Definition and essence of defamation. Defamation may be defined as "a statement concerning any person which exposes him to hatred, ridicule or contempt or which causes him to be shunned or avoided or which has a tendency to injure him in his office, profession or trade": *see Myroft* v. *Sleight* (1921).

(*a*) The statement is judged in relation to the standards of right-thinking members of society.

(*b*) Mere insult or vulgar abuse is not defamation: *Parkins* v. *Scott* (1862).

(*c*) What is defamatory at one point in time may cease to be defamatory at another. *See Slazengers Ltd.* v. *Gibbs & Co.* (1916); *Braddock* v. *Bevins* (1948).

(*d*) A statement may be defamatory even though no person believes it to be true: *Theaker* v. *Richardson* (1962).

(*e*) Defamation may take the form of libel or slander (*see* **25–26** below).

25. Libel. Libel consists of a defamatory statement made in a visible or permanent form, e.g. writing, pictures, effigies (*see Monson* v. *Tussauds* (1894)). *See Desmond* v. *Thorne* (1982).

(*a*) Libel may be not only a tort, but also a criminal offence if it tends to provoke a breach of the peace.

(*b*) Libel is actionable *per se*, i.e. without proof of special damage.

(*c*) The words may not be defamatory in themselves, but when considered in the context of extrinsic circumstance they may be defamatory. In that case, the plaintiff will plead an "innuendo", i.e. that the words have a secondary, defamatory meaning. *See Hayward* v. *Thompson* (1982).

26. Slander. Slander consists of defamatory, spoken statements or gestures.

(*a*) Slander is a tort only, not a crime.

(*b*) Slander is actionable only on proof of special damage, save, for example, where the words suggest that the plaintiff is suffering from a contagious disease, or where they are calculated to disparage him in his office, profession or business or where they impute to him a crime carrying a sentence of imprisonment.

27. Defences. The defendant may plead the following defences:

(*a*) *Justification*, i.e. that the statement complained of was true: *see Beevis* v. *Dawson* (1957).

(*b*) *Fair comment*, i.e. that the statement complained of was fair comment on a matter of public interest: *see Kemsley* v. *Foot* (1951).

(*c*) *Consent*, i.e. that the plaintiff has consented expressly or impliedly to publication.

(*d*) *Absolute privilege*. A statement which is absolutely privileged may not be used as the basis for an action for defamation, no matter whether it be false, defamatory, or made from malice. Such statements include those made: by a judge in the course of proceedings; in Parliament by a member; between husband and wife.

(*e*) *Qualified privilege*. Where a statement attracts qualified privilege, then if it has been made honestly and without malice, it will not become the basis of an action for defamation. Qualified privilege applies to: statements made in the performance of a duty; statements made in the protection of an interest; reports of parliamentary, judicial and some other types of proceedings (*see* Defamation Act 1952, s. 7); professional communications between solicitor and client. *See Blackshaw* v. *Lord* (1983).

PROGRESS TEST 16

1. What is a tort? **(1)**
2. Explain vicarious liability. **(2)**
3. Explain *volenti non fit injuria* **(4)**
4. Define and illustrate the tort of negligence. **(7)**
5. Explain *res ipsa loquitur*. **(9)**
6. What is the difference between public and private nuisance? **(12, 13)**
7. Explain trespass to the person. **(17)**
8. What is the rule in *Rylands* v. *Fletcher* (1868)? **(19)**
9. Define defamation. **(24)**
10. Explain libel and slander. **(25, 26)**

CHAPTER XVII

Civil Law (3): Land Law; Trusts

INTRODUCTORY MATTERS

1. The concept of land. Land has a specific, technical meaning in law. It was defined by Coke as comprehending "any ground, soil or earth whatsoever, as meadows, pastures, woods, moors, waters, marshes, furzes and heaths. . . . It legally includeth also all castles, houses, and other buildings." In modern law, land includes not only the physical surface of the earth, but also buildings, minerals, etc. *See*, for a full definition, Law of Property Act 1925, s. 205(1)(*ix*).

2. The concept of a trust. Assume that S conveys property (Blackacre) to T, directing T to hold it "on trust" for B. The essence of this transaction is the confidence reposed in T by S; the resulting obligation binds T so that he will not generally be permitted to depart from his undertaking. In this example: S is the *settlor*; T is the *trustee*; B is the *beneficiary*; Blackacre is the *trust property*; T's obligation is the *basis of the trust*.

3. Matters to be discussed. The following topics are touched upon in this chapter:

    (*a*) some fundamentals of land law, i.e. estates and tenures (*see* **5–7** below);

    (*b*) the nature of incumbrances on land (*see* **8–16** below);

    (*c*) some fundamentals of the law of trusts (*see* **17–21** below);

    (*d*) matters relating to trustees and variation of trusts (*see* **22–26** below);

SOME FUNDAMENTALS OF LAND LAW

4. Preliminary matters. For long periods in our history, he who owned the land possessed decisive economic and political power. The feudal system was based on ownership of land and the duties arising therefrom. Ownership, possession and transfer of land became vital factors in the development of land law. Today, that law reflects its feudal parentage in its terminology and, perhaps above all, in its concepts of tenure and estate. *Tenure* is concerned with the problem: upon what terms is land held? The matter is of limited significance today; feudal tenures have disappeared. Freehold and leasehold systems of tenure remain of importance. *Estate* is concerned with the problem: for how long is land held?

5. The concept of the estate. "Tenure" relates to conditions under which land is held; "estate" applies to the *length of the period of time* for which a person is entitled to hold the land. "All estates are but times of their continuances": Bacon.

6. Classification of estates. At common law the following estates were recognised: *freehold estates*, i.e. estates whose duration is not known (e.g. estate in fee simple, in fee tail, for life, *pur autre vie*); less-than-freehold estates, i.e. estates where the duration is certain (e.g. leaseholds for a fixed term of years, tenancies from year to year).

(*a*) *Fee simple estate.* This is the largest estate in terms of duration. It may be "fee simple absolute in possession". Fee (*feudum* = a fief) indicates that the estate can be inherited. *Simple* indicates that there are no restrictions as to whom the fee may pass. *Absolute* means that the estate is not subject to determination by any event other than that implied or stated in the grant. *In possession* means that the estate is immediate. A grant of land "to X and his heirs in fee simple" means that the estate endures for as long as the person entitled at any time has an heir.

(*b*) *Fee tail* (*taillé* = cut). This is an estate which may be inherited only by specified descendants of the original grantee.

(*c*) *Estate for life.* This estate is held by the grantee for his life.

(*d*) *Estate pur autre vie* ("for the life of another"). This type of estate was created where there was a grant of land "to X for the life of Y". Here, X held the land only so long as Y lived.

7. Freeholds and leaseholds. These classifications of estates are based on the following concepts:

(*a*) The freehold approximates, in effect, to absolute ownership. It involves a fee simple estate in land.

(*b*) The leasehold (which is "an estate less than freehold") involves a landlord (or lessor) who owns the land, and a tenant (or lessee) to whom possession of land is given, usually for a stated period of time under the terms of a lease. When the lease comes to an end the land reverts to the landlord.

(*c*) Estates in land may subsist concurrently. Assume that L, who owns the fee simple in Blackacre, grants a lease to T, and that T makes a sub-lease to X. In such a case there are three estates in Blackacre existing concurrently.

INCUMBRANCES ON LAND

8. Preliminary matters. In practice the owner of land has a less than absolute freedom over his land. Statutory restrictions, for example (*see* the Town and Country Planning Acts 1947–84), are numerous; others may have rights of way over his land. The following incumbrances are considered below:

    (*a*) easements and *profits à prendre* (*see* **9–10** below);

    (*b*) restrictive covenants (*see* **11** below);

    (*c*) mortgages (*see* **12–16** below).

9. Easements. An easement is a right which one person possesses in the land of another. Essentially, it is a right capable of forming the subject-matter of a grant which is appurtenant to the land of one person and exercisable over the land of another.

    (*a*) *Examples of easements*: rights of way (*see Cousens* v. *Rose* (1871)); rights of water (*see Baxendale* v. *McMurray* (1867)); the use of a wall for fixing a sign (*see Moody* v. *Steggles* (1879)).

    (*b*) *Terminology.* Assume that A, owner of Blackacre, grants B, owner of the adjoining Whiteacre, the right to walk across Blackacre. The right of way thus granted is in the nature of an *easement*. Blackacre is the *servient tenement*; Whiteacre is the *dominant tenement*. A is the *servient owner*; B is the *dominant owner*. The easement is an *affirmative easement*, i.e. A must allow B to perform an act (of walking) upon the servient tenement.

    (*c*) *A right over the land of another is not necessarily an easement.* A right is an easement only where it has the following qualities: there must be a dominant and a servient tenement; each must be owned by a different person; the easement must accommodate the dominant tenement; the right must be capable of being granted by deed.

10. Profit à prendre. This is a right to take something off another's land, as where X has a right to cut and take turf on Y's land. *See Lady Dunsany* v. *Bedworth* (1979).

11. Restrictive covenants. Assume that X owns and occupies Blackacre and that he sells part of Blackacre in fee simple to Y. X and Y agree that Y shall not use his part of Blackacre for, say, any purposes connected with the manufacturing industry. Y is the *convenantor*; X is the *covenantee*. The contract is in the nature of a *restrictive covenant*, i.e. a contract whereby one owner of land (Y) agrees to restrict the use of his land for the benefit of another owner of land (X). The part of Blackacre retained by X is the *dominant land*; the part bought by Y is the *servient land*.

(*a*) The general position at common law was that the benefit of a positive or negative covenant could be enforced by an assignee of the original covenantee (so that, in the example above, if X had assigned a covenant to A, then A would have been entitled to enforce that covenant). The rule operated only if: the covenant touched and concerned the covenantee's land; the covenantee had the legal estate in the land to be benefited; the person wishing to enforce the covenant had the same estate as that possessed by the original covenantee.

(*b*) The rule in equity is that the purchaser of land who has notice of a restrictive covenant affecting that land may be restrained from use of the land which is not consistent with that covenant: *Tulk* v. *Moxhay* (1848). The rule applies only if: the covenant is negative in substance; the covenantee has retained land intended to be protected by the covenant; the assignee of the dominant land can show that he has acquired the benefit of the covenant. *See Windsor Hotel* v. *Allan* (1981).

12. Mortgages: the general concept. A mortgage arises where property is conveyed so that repayment of a debt or the discharge of some other obligation is assured. Assume that A borrows money from B and that he later conveys property to B as a security for repayment of the loan. The *mortgage* is the conveyance of property by A to B; A is the *mortgagor*; B is the *mortgagee*. The debt for which security has been created is the *mortgage debt*. The date which is specified in the mortgage deed as being that on which A will repay the principal plus interest is the *date of redemption*.

13. The equity of redemption. Immediately a mortgage is created, the mortgagor acquires a contractual right to redeem on the date of redemption and, after that date has passed, an equitable right to redeem. Together, these rights constitute A's *equity of redemption*. The right of redemption is inviolable; it may be postponed, but it cannot be restricted unduly; the right may, nevertheless, be lost, e.g. by foreclosure or release of the equity. *See Knightsbridge Estates Ltd.* v. *Byrne* (1940).

14. Discharge of a mortgage. A mortgage may be discharged by foreclosure (by court order); by redemption; by the mortgagee exercising his power of sale.

15. Rights of the mortgagor. Generally the mortgagor has the following rights: to redeem; to enjoy the property; to grant leases; to accept surrender of leases; to bring actions; to require the mortgagee to transfer the mortgage to a third party.

16. Rights of the mortgagee. Generally the mortgagee has the following rights: to foreclose; to take possession; to exercise power of sale when the legal date for redemption has passed; to appoint a receiver; to grant and accept surrender of leases.

SOME FUNDAMENTALS OF THE TRUST

17. Preliminary matters. *See* **2** above. The main reasons for the employment of the trust today include: where people wish to hold land jointly, the trust is a useful instrument; the incidence of taxation may be reduced by the use of a trust in some cases; where people wish to provide for interests to arise at a future time or wish to guard family property against the excesses of a spendthrift, a trust may be employed.

18. Definition of a trust. Sir Arthur Underhill's definition was expressly approved in *Green* v. *Russell* (1959): "An equitable obligation binding a person (who is called a trustee) to deal with property over which he has control (which is called the trust property), for the benefit of persons (who are called beneficiaries . . .), of whom he may himself be one, and any one of whom may enforce the obligation. Any act or neglect on the part of a trustee which is not authorised or excused by the terms of the trust instrument, or by law, is called a breach of trust."

19. Types of trust (1). The following should be noted:

(*a*) *Trusts imposed by statute.* Examples: under the Administration of Estates Act 1925, s. 33, the property of an intestate (*see* XVIII, **20**) will vest in his personal representatives upon trust for sale; under the Law of Property Act 1925, s. 36, where a legal estate is held in trust for persons as joint tenants, it is to be held on trust for sale.

(*b*) *Express (or "declared") trusts.* An express trust is one created by intentional and express declaration of the settlor. Example: X, by his will, devises Blackacre to Y "in trust for Z".

(*c*) *Implied, resulting and constructive trusts.* An *implied trust* is one which arises out of the settlor's presumed, but unexpressed, intention. Example: X agrees with Y, for value, to convey an estate to him; X is then deemed to be a trustee of that estate for Y. A *resulting trust* (*resultare* = to spring back) exists as a consequence of a reversion of property to the settlor, by operation of equity. Example: X conveys property to Y on trust for Z who, in fact, is dead. There is a resulting trust of the beneficial estate in its entirety to X. A *constructive trust* arises by operation of equity from an existing fiduciary relationship between parties. Example: a trustee of a lease obtained a renewal for his own benefit. He was directed to hold the new lease upon the same trusts as he had held that which had expired: *Keech* v. *Sandford*

(1726). *See Peffer* v. *Rigg* (1977); *Universe Tankships* v. *I.T.W.F.* (1982).

20. Types of trust (2). The following further types should be noted:

(*a*) *Executory and executed trusts.* An *executory trust* arises where the settlor has created a valid trust, but where some further instrument is necessary in order to define the interests arising from the trust. Example: A gives property to B in trust to "cause it to be settled on C in strict settlement". An *executed trust* arises where the trust is completely and finally declared and no further instrument is needed to define the limitations. Example: A vests property in B on trust "for C for life and, on C's death, for D absolutely". *See Miles* v. *Harford* (1879); *Re Bostock's Settlement* (1921).

(*b*) *Completely and incompletely constituted trusts.* A *completely constituted trust* is one in which the trust property has been completely vested in the trustees. Example: X vests the trust property in Y and Z, the trustees, upon the requisite trusts. An *incompletely constituted trust* is one in which the trust property has not been vested in the trustees. Example: an intending donor executed a transfer of shares, but died before the necessary Treasury consent could be given. No confirmatory transfer had been given and the trust was held to be incompletely constituted: *Re Fry* (1946). *See Swiss Bank Ltd.* v. *Lloyds Bank Ltd.* (1980).

(*c*) *Simple and special trusts.* A *simple trust* is one in which the trustee has no important active duties to perform. Example: X devises property to Y in trust for Z. Y's sole duty is to convey the legal estate to Z. A *special trust* is one in which a trustee is appointed in order to carry out some scheme designated by the settlor. Example: X's task as trustee involves the task of collecting rents and paying them to the beneficiary.

(*d*) *Private and public trusts.* A *private trust* is for the benefit of an individual or class. Example: X devises property to Y in trust for Y's son Z. A *public* (*or "charitable"*) *trust* has as its object the promotion of the public welfare. Example: X creates a trust for the relief of poverty. (*See* further, **21** below).

21. Charitable trusts. Trusts of this type are characterised by their terms, under which the income is to be applied exclusively for purposes of a charitable nature. They must be, if they are to be upheld as charitable trusts, wholly and exclusively charitable and must promote some public benefit.

(*a*) The preamble to the Statute of Charitable Uses 1601 remains a guide today to the principles upon which the question of the charitable nature of a trust may be decided.

(*b*) The investment income of a charitable trust is generally exempt from income tax if it is applied only for charitable purposes; its trading income may be exempt similarly if applied only for charitable purposes *and* if the purpose of the charity is to carry on such work.

(*c*) A private trust may fail if there is no certainty as to ascertainable beneficiaries (*see Re Endacott* (1960)), but in the case of a charitable trust there will be no failure provided that there is certainty of intention to give property to charity and that such intention is exclusively charitable (i.e. that its essential nature comes within the court's interpretation of the application of the 1601 statute).

(*d*) "Charity" is defined in the Charities Act 1960, s. 45(1), as meaning "any institution, corporate or not, which is established for charitable purposes and is subject to the control of the High Court in the exercise of the court's jurisdiction with respect to charities". *See Incorporated Society of Law Reporting* v. *A.-G.* (1971); *Construction I.T.B.* v. *A.-G.* (1972).

(*e*) The generally-accepted classification of charitable trusts is based on *Pemsel's Case* (1891): trusts for the relief of poverty, the advancement of religion, the advancement of education and other purposes beneficial to the community.

(*f*) If a charitable trust is impracticable initially, or becomes so subsequently, it will not necessarily fail; its property may be applied *cy-près* (= as near) to some other charitable purpose which resembles the original purpose as nearly as possible. *See* Charities Act 1960, ss. 13, 14; *Re Lysaght* (1966); *Liverpool & District Hospital* v. *A.-G.* (1981).

TRUSTEES AND VARIATION OF TRUSTS

22. Preliminaries. *See* **2** above. In general, the capacity to be a trustee exists wherever there is the capacity to take and possess property. Any person may be a beneficiary. In general, any number of persons may be appointed as trustees; in the case of a settlement of land held on trust for sale, the maximum number is four. *See* Trustee Act 1925, s. 34(1), (2).

23. Appointment of trustees. Trustees may be appointed by the settlor, under express power conferred by the trust instrument, under the Trustee Act 1925, s. 36 (e.g. where a trustee desires to be discharged), or by the court. Acceptance of office may be express or presumed: *Re Sharman's Will Trusts* (1942); there can be no renunciation after acceptance.

24. Termination of trusteeship. A trustee can retire only under an express power of appointing new trustees, under statutory power conferred by the Trustee Act 1925, s. 39, by order of the court (e.g. as where he has behaved improperly in relation to the trust), or by consent of all the beneficiaries.

25. Duties of the trustee. His principal duties relate to: acquainting himself with the terms of the trust, e.g. by inspection of the trust instrument; acting in the discharge of his duties and in the exercise of his discretion with diligence; acting gratuitously and not profiting from the trust; not delegating his powers or duties; acting unanimously with co-trustees; investing only in securities authorised by the settlement or by statute (*see* Trustee Investments Act 1961); acting impartially as between beneficiaries; not deviating from the terms of the trust. *See Boardman* v. *Phipps* (1966).

26. Variation of trusts. Under the Variation of Trusts Act 1958, s. 1(1), the court may, if it thinks fit, by order, approve any arrangement varying or revoking all or any of the trusts on behalf of persons having an interest in the trusts, but who are incapable of assenting, or persons who may become entitled or persons unborn. *See Re Steed's W.T.* (1960); *Re Remnant's S.T.* (1970).

PROGRESS TEST 17

1. Explain the concept of land in English law. **(1)**
2. Explain the terms "settlor", "trustee", "beneficiary" in relation to a trust. **(2)**
3. What is meant in land law by "estate"? **(4)**
4. Explain "fee simple absolute in possession". **(6)**
5. Explain *estate pur autre vie*. **(6)**
6. What is a leasehold? **(7)**
7. Explain the nature of an easement. **(9)**
8. What are *profits à prendre*? **(10)**
9. What is a restrictive covenant? **(11)**
10. Explain "equity of redemption". **(13)**
11. What are the rights of a mortgagor? **(15)**
12. What is an express trust? **(19)**
13. Give examples of implied and resulting trusts. **(19)**
14. Explain the nature of a charitable trust. **(21)**
15. What are the main duties of a trustee? **(25)**

CHAPTER XVIII

Other Aspects of Law (1): Family Law

INTRODUCTORY MATTERS

1. Background and content of family law. Much of the earlier law relating to the family fell within the jurisdiction of the ecclesiastical courts. Marriage and its legal consequences were related essentially to church doctrine and its interpretation. Until 1857 the ecclesiastical courts possessed an exclusive jurisdiction over matrimonial disputes. The Matrimonial Causes Act 1857 created the Divorce Court which was given the powers formerly exercised by the ecclesiastical courts and, additionally, was empowered to dissolve marriage in some few circumstances. The recent growth of the welfare state, the development of secular attitudes to the marriage ceremony and the increasing concern for the welfare of children have resulted in a vast extension of the area of family law. Its province includes the following areas, for example:

(*a*) formalities of marriage (*see* **2** below);
(*b*) nullity of marriage (*see* **5–8** below);
(*c*) dissolution of marriage (*see* **9–10** below);
(*d*) legitimacy and allied matters (*see* **11–13** below);
(*e*) adoption (*see* **14–15** below);
(*f*) matters relating to the disposition of property on death (*see* **16–21** below).

2. Births, marriages and deaths: legal formalities. The law requires the registration of every birth, marriage and death. In the case of a *birth*, registration must be completed within forty-two days. It consists of furnishing particulars, such as: date, place of birth, name, surname and sex of child, particulars of parents. *See* Births and Deaths Registration Act 1953. In the case of a *marriage*, the formalities depend on whether it is to be celebrated inside or outside the Church of England. If inside, the wedding is preceded by the reading of banns on three successive Sundays in a parish church. A licence may be required and, additionally, a certificate from the superintendent registrar. Marriage outside the Church of England requires a certificate and, in some cases, a licence. *See* Marriage Acts 1949–83. In the case of *death*, there must be furnished within three to four days, particulars of: date, place and cause of death, particulars of addresses and occupation of deceased, etc.

3. The concept of marriage in law. Marriage is seen as an act or rite based on a consensual union which creates the legal status of husband and wife. "The voluntary union for life of one man and one woman to the exclusion of all others": *see* Matrimonial Causes Act 1857. The minimum age of the parties is sixteen: Marriage Act 1969. There are prohibited degrees of relationship within which a marriage is void, e.g. a man and his aunt. *See Hyde v. Hyde* (1866); *Silver v. Silver* (1955).

4. Problems of succession. The disposition of a person's property on his death is now governed strictly by statute. These matters are discussed at **16–21** below.

NULLITY OF MARRIAGE

5. Preliminary matters. Church doctrine, which taught that a valid marriage could be terminated only by death, was tempered by its awareness that a marriage might be declared null and void if it could be shown never to have been a "perfect marriage", i.e. if there had been no marriage at all. The law relating to nullity has now developed and is contained within the Matrimonial Causes Act 1973. A decree of divorce (*see* **9** below) ends a valid marriage: a decree of nullity declares that the marriage never has been—in the widest sense—valid.

6. Void marriages. A void marriage "is one that will be regarded by every court in any case in which the existence of the marriage is in issue as never having taken place and can be so treated by both parties to it without the necessity of any decree annulling it": *per* Lord Greene in *De Reneville v. De Reneville* (1948). The grounds upon which a marriage will be held to be void are stated in the Matrimonial Causes Act 1973, s. 11, thus:

(*a*) that it is not a valid marriage under the provisions of the Marriage Acts 1949–70 (that is to say where:

(*i*) the parties are within the prohibited degrees of relationship (*see* Marriage Act 1949, s. 1(1) and Matrimonial Causes Act 1973, s. 11(*a*));

(*ii*) either party is under the age of sixteen;

(*iii*) the parties have intermarried in disregard of certain requirements as to the formation of marriage);

(*b*) that at the time of the marriage either party was already lawfully married.

7. Voidable marriages. A voidable marriage "is one that will be regarded by every court as a valid subsisting marriage until a decree annulling it has been pronounced by a court of competent jurisdiction": *per* Lord Greene in *De Reneville* v. *De Reneville* (1948). The grounds upon which a marriage will be held to be voidable are set out in the Matrimonial Causes Act 1973, s. 12, as follows:

(*a*) that the marriage has not been consummated owing to the incapacity of either party to consummate it, or the wilful refusal of the respondent [the person against whom the petition is being presented] to consummate it;

(*b*) that either party to the marriage did not validly consent, because of, e.g. mistake, unsoundness of mind;

(*c*) that at the time of the marriage either party was suffering from mental disorder of such a kind as to be unfitted for marriage;

(*d*) that at the time of the marriage the respondent was suffering from venereal disease in a communicable form, or was pregnant by some person other than the petitioner.

8. Bars to relief in the case of a voidable marriage. The court will not generally grant a decree of nullity on the grounds that a marriage is voidable where the respondent satisfies the court that the petitioner, with knowledge that it was open to him to have the marriage avoided, so conducted himself in relation to the respondent as to lead the respondent reasonably to believe that he would not seek to do so and that it would be unjust to the respondent to grant the decree.

DISSOLUTION OF MARRIAGE

9. Preliminary matters. Until 1971, divorce, i.e. the dissolution of marriage, depended on the petitioner proving a matrimonial offence, e.g. adultery, cruelty, desertion. Under the Matrimonial Causes Act 1973, s. 1(1) "a petition for divorce may be presented to the court by either party to a marriage on the ground that the marriage has broken down irretrievably". In such a case, where the court is satisfied of such a breakdown, a decree of divorce is granted.

10. Evidence of irretrievable breakdown. The following facts are considered to be evidence of irretrievable breakdown of marriage (*see* Matrimonial Causes Act 1973, s. 1):

(*a*) that the respondent has committed adultery and the petitioner finds it intolerable to live with the respondent;

(*b*) that the respondent has behaved in such a way that the petitioner cannot reasonably be expected to live with the respondent;

(*c*) that the respondent has deserted the petitioner for a continuous period of at least two years immediately preceding presentation of the petition;

(*d*) that the parties to the marriage have lived apart for a continuous period of at least two years immediately preceding the presentation of the petition and the respondent consents to a decree being granted;

(*e*) that the parties to the marriage have lived apart for a continuous period of at least five years immediately preceding presentation of the petition.

LEGITIMACY AND ALLIED MATTERS

11. Preliminary matters. Many matters concerning the relationship, rights and duties of parent and child, are based on the legitimate or illegitimate nature of that relationship. A child born to parents married to one another is presumed to be their legitimate child: *Gardner* v. *Gardner* (1877).

(*a*) *Children of voidable marriages.* If celebrated before July 1971, a child who would have been the legitimate child of the parties to the marriage if at the date of decree of nullity it had been dissolved instead of annulled, is deemed to be their legitimate child; if celebrated after that date, children conceived before the decree absolute are legitimate. *See* Matrimonial Causes Act 1973, s. 16.

(*b*) *Children of void marriages.* Children are legitimate if at the time of intercourse resulting in their birth (or time of celebration of marriage, if later) both or either of the parties reasonably believed the marriage was valid: Legitimacy Act 1976, s. 1.

12. Legitimation. This is a procedure whereby a child is treated as legitimate following the subsequent marriage of its parents. Where the parents of an illegitimate child marry one another, the marriage shall, if the father of the illegitimate person is at the date of the marriage domiciled in England and Wales, render that person, if living, legitimate from the date of the marriage: Legitimacy Act 1976, s. 2. *See* also Children Act 1975, s. 8(9).

13. The illegitimate child. The fundamental differences in law between legitimate and illegitimate children are gradually disappearing. *See* Family Law Reform Act 1969; Fatal Accidents Act 1976, s. 1(4). "Whatever may have been the position in the past, the general attitude towards illegitimacy has changed and the legitimate incidents of being born a bastard are now almost non-existent": *S.* v. *S.* (1972). Note that an *affiliation order* may be issued by a court, finding or declaring a person to be the father of a child and providing for its maintenance. Proceedings can be instituted by the mother, or a local authority or custodian of the child. *See* Affiliation Proceedings Act 1957, as amended; Children Act 1975, s. 45.

ADOPTION

14. Preliminary matters. The law allows, under carefully defined and controlled conditions, the vesting of rights and duties of a parent in relation to children in some other person, i.e. the adopter. The procedure is known as adoption and is regulated by the Adoption Acts 1958–76 and the Children Act 1975. (*See* also Child Care Act 1980; Adoption Rules (S.I. 1984/265).)

15. General rules relating to adoption. The following should be noted:

(*a*) An adoption order may be made by the Family Division, county court or magistrates' court. Prime consideration must be given to the child's long-term welfare before the order is made: Adoption Act 1976, s. 6. An order is not generally made unless the child is free for adoption: s. 16(1).

(*b*) A body or person other than an approved adoption agency or a relative of the child or a person acting in pursuance of a High Court order cannot make arrangements for adoptions: s. 11(1).

(*c*) A register relating to adoption orders is maintained by the Registrar-General; any person may search the index: s. 50.

(*d*) An adopted child is treated in law, where the adopters are a married couple, as if he had been born a child of the marriage and, in any other case, as if he had been born to the adopter in wedlock, and as if he were not the child of any person other than the adopters: Adoption Act 1976, s. 30.

PRINCIPLES OF THE LAW OF SUCCESSION

16. Preliminary matters. The law of succession is concerned with the problems which may arise on the disposition and devolution of property on the death of the owner. In particular, problems arise where the owner lacks the capacity to make a will, or has failed to make a will, or has not made reasonable provision for the maintenance of a spouse.

17. Wills: the general principles. A will is a revocable declaration, made in the prescribed form, of the maker's intentions concerning the disposition and devolution of his property, and other matters, which he desires shall become effective on and after the event of his death. A will: is no more than a declaration of its maker's intentions; is invariably revocable (i.e. the maker can always cancel it); is invariably ambulatory (i.e. it "speaks only from the death of the testator");

becomes effective only on the testator's death; must generally be in the form prescribed by statute. If the court is satisfied that a will is so expressed that it fails to carry out the maker's intentions because of a clerical error or failure to understand his instructions, the court may order the will to be rectified: Administration of Justice Act 1982, s. 22(1); *see Re Reynette-James* (1976); *Re Lewis' WT* (1984).

18. Wills: formalities. Formalities are governed largely by the Wills Acts 1837–1968.

(*a*) Any property vested in the testator at his death may be disposed of by his will.

(*b*) Any person may receive benefits under a will. Special rules apply to witnesses and executors.

(*c*) Every person is deemed to have the power of testamentary disposition (*see* Wills Act 1837, s. 3). There are exceptions in the case of minors (*see* Wills Act 1837, s. 7; Family Law Reform Act 1969, s. 3(1)) and testators of unsound mind.

(*d*) A will made without *animus testandi* (i.e. the true desire to make a will) is generally invalid.

"No will shall be valid unless:

(*a*) it is in writing and signed by the testator, or by some other person in his presence and by his direction; and

(*b*) it appears that the testator intended by his signature to give effect to the will; and

(*c*) the signature is made or acknowledged by the testator in the presence of two or more witnesses present at the same time; and

(*d*) each witness either

(*i*) attests and signs the will; or

(*ii*) acknowledges his signature, in the presence of the testator (but not necessarily in the presence of any other witness), but no form of attestation shall be necessary"; Wills Act 1837, s. 9, substituted by Administration of Justice Act 1982, s. 17.

19. Probate. Probate is a document issued under seal of the court as official evidence of the authority of an executor, i.e. one appointed by will to administer the testator's property. If the validity of a will is contested, probate is granted only after the court has pronounced in favour: this is known as grant of probate in solemn form.

20. Intestacy. Where a deceased person has died wholly intestate, i.e. having left no will, or having left a will which is totally ineffective, the devolution of his property is governed by the Administration of Estates Act 1925, as amended by the Intestates' Estates Act 1952.

(*a*) On the death of a person intestate, his estate is to be held by his personal representatives, "as to the real estate upon trust to sell the same; and as to the personal estate upon trust to call in, sell and convert into money such part thereof as may not consist of money": Administration of Estates Act 1925, s. 53(1) (*b*).

(*b*) The mode of distribution of the intestate's estate will depend on whether he does or does not leave a surviving spouse: *see* Administration of Estates Act 1925, s. 46.

21. Provision for family and dependants. This matter is now regulated by the Inheritance (Provision for Family and Dependants) Act 1975. Where, after commencement of the Act, a person dies domiciled in England and Wales and is survived by any of the persons mentioned at (*a*) below, that person may apply to the court for an order under s. 2 of the Act on the ground that the disposition of the deceased's estate effected by his will or the law relating to intestacy, or the combination of his will and that law, is not such as to make reasonable financial provision for the applicant.

(*a*) Persons who may apply include: wife or husband of the deceased; former wife or former husband of the deceased who has not remarried; a child of the deceased; any person (not being a child of the deceased) who, in the case of any marriage to which the deceased was at any time a party, was treated by the deceased as a child of the family in relation to that marriage; any person (not being included in the above-mentioned categories) who immediately before the death of the deceased was being maintained either wholly or partly by the deceased. *See Re Wilkinson* (1977); *Re Rowlands* (1984).

(*b*) "Reasonable financial provision" means such financial provision as it would be reasonable in all the circumstances of the case for a husband or wife to receive, whether or not that provision is required for his or her maintenance, or such provision as it would be reasonable in all the circumstances of the case for another applicant to receive for his maintenance.

PROGRESS TEST 18

1. What is the concept of marriage in English law? **(3)**
2. What is the difference between a void and a voidable marriage? **(6, 7)**
3. On what grounds is a marriage voidable? **(7)**
4. Outline the bars to relief in the case of a voidable marriage. **(8)**
5. What is the sole ground today for presentation of a petition for divorce? **(9)**
6. Explain "legitimation". **(12)**
7. What is an affiliation order? **(13)**
8. Enumerate some of the main rules relating to adoption. **(15)**

9. Is a will always revocable before the testator's death? **(17)**

10. Does a will always require attestation? **(18)**

11. Outline some of the effects of the recent legislation relating to provision for a testator's family and dependants. **(21)**

CHAPTER XIX

Other Aspects of Law (2): Employment Law

INTRODUCTORY MATTERS

1. Essence of employment law. Employment law, known also as "labour law", is concerned with the circumstances surrounding the relationship of employer and employee. Traditionally, the state took little interest in these matters. The Statute of Artificers 1563 was an early example of state intervention in matters such as wages and apprenticeships. The Industrial Revolution and the era of *laissez-faire* reflected the belief that state intervention should be as infrequent as possible and that contracts between employer and employee should be based on free bargaining. But the social problems created by industrial growth and the spread of trade unions led to a changed attitude. Today the state intervenes directly in matters related to employment and this is evident in the topics selected for discussion in this chapter:

  (*a*) the contract of employment (*see* **3–6** below);
  (*b*) common law doctrines of employment (*see* **7–8** below);
  (*c*) dismissal from employment (*see* **9–16** below);
  (*d*) matters arising under recent legislation (*see* **17–20** below);
  (*e*) discrimination in employment (*see* **21–23** below);
  (*f*) trade unions (*see* **24–28** below).

2. Characteristics of employment law. Employment law is an amalgam of matters relating to contract, tort and criminal law. It is based on common law and legislation, but in recent years state intervention in matters such as collective bargaining and the closed shop has appeared. Thus, the Industrial Relations Act 1971 (repealed in 1974) aimed at transforming a part of the voluntary basis of industrial relations into a system based on legal control. It attempted to set a pattern of state intervention which now characterises, in growing measure, some sections of employment law.

THE CONTRACT OF EMPLOYMENT

3. Preliminaries. It is important to note that the contract of employment need not be in written form (unless the employee is an apprentice). However, under the Contracts of Employment Act 1972, as embodied in the Employment Protection (Consolidation) Act 1978, an employer is required to provide his employee with a written statement (not a contract) setting out the main terms and conditions of employment, within thirteen weeks of the employee starting work. (The statement can be used as evidence of the terms and conditions forming an oral contract of employment.) *See System Floors Ltd.* v. *Daniel* (1982).

4. Definition of an employee. Under statute, an employee is "an individual who has entered into or works under (or, where the employment has ceased, worked under) a contract with an employer, whether the contract be for manual labour, clerical work or otherwise, be expressed or implied, oral or in writing, and whether it be a contract of service or apprenticeship". *See* Employment Protection (Consolidation) Act 1978, s. 153 (1); *Nethermere Ltd* v. *Gardiner* (1983).

5. Written terms of employment. Written terms must be given to all employees except, for example, those employed for less than sixteen hours a week, Crown servants, or an employee who is the employer's spouse. The terms must include: details of scale rate, or method of calculating remuneration; intervals at which remuneration is paid; terms relating to hours of work, holidays, sickness, length of notice, title of job; disciplinary rules, etc. *See* 1978 Act, s. 2.

6. Right to period of notice. An employer must give an employee at least one week's notice if the employee has been employed by him continuously for four weeks or more; at least two weeks' notice if the employee has been employed by him continuously for two years or more; one additional week's notice for each further complete year of continuous employment up to twelve weeks' notice if the employee has been employed by him continuously for twelve years or more. An employee must give his employer at least one week's notice if he has been employed by him continuously for four weeks or more; the period of notice does not increase with longer service. *See* 1978 Act, s. 49.

COMMON LAW DUTIES OF EMPLOYER AND EMPLOYEE

7. Duties of the employer. Under common law, the employer was held to have the following duties: to pay the agreed remuneration; to provide work; to care for the worker's physical safety; to indemnify the employee in respect of liabilities and expenses incurred by him in carrying out his employer's orders.

8. Duties of the employee. Under common law, the employee was held to have the following duties: to perform satisfactorily work given to him by his employer; to obey, and show good faith to, his employer.

DISMISSAL

9. Preliminaries. Statute has interfered with the unfettered right of an employer to dismiss an employee. Under the 1978 Act, for example, a right is given to employees not to be dismissed "unfairly". An employee who thinks that he has been unfairly dismissed may seek a remedy through complaint to an industrial tribunal.

10. Meaning of "dismissal". Under the Trade Union and Labour Relations Act 1974, dismissal means the termination of an employee's contract of employment by his employer, with or without notice, or by the employee himself (because of his employer's conduct). Note that an employee is generally regarded as having been dismissed where he is employed under a fixed-term contract and that contract is not renewed on expiry of that term. (*See* Employment Act 1980.)

11. Who may complain. A complaint may be made by an employee who is dismissed, but not by, for example, an independent contractor, part-time employees, employees who, before the effective date of termination of employment, had reached retirement age.

12. Fair dismissal. Under the 1978 Act, dismissal may be regarded as "fair" if it arises because of: the employee's conduct; redundancy; lack of capability or qualifications for the job, a contravention of the law which might result from his continued employment; some other substantial reason.

13. Unfair dismissal. A dismissal is considered "unfair" if, for example, the main reason is that: the employee was a member of, or proposed to join, an independent trade union (*see* **26** below); or had taken part, or proposed to take part, at an appropriate time, in the activities of an independent union; or refused to belong to a non-independent union; or has been unfairly selected for redundancy; or has been selected for dismissal from among those taking part in a strike while others have been re-engaged. *See* Employment Act 1980, s. 4; Employment Act 1982, ss. 2–9; *Woods* v. *W. M. Car Services Ltd* (1982).

14. Complaint to an industrial tribunal. An employee who considers that he has been unfairly dismissed can complain to an industrial tribunal after a conciliation officer has had an opportunity to consider whether a settlement can be reached. A tribunal has no jurisdiction to investigate "fairness of dismissal" if, e.g., the employee has not been employed continuously for one year, or two years in the case of a business with twenty or fewer employees. *See* Employment Act 1982, s. 20.

15. Remedies for unfair dismissal. A tribunal can order *reinstatement* (i.e. the employee's return to his former job on similar terms and conditions) or *re-engagement* (i.e. re-employment, but not necessarily in the same job or on similar terms and conditions). An alternative remedy of *compensation* may be awarded if either party refuses to comply with the tribunal's recommendation, or the recommendation is impracticable to carry out or is not equitable in its effect.

16. Redundancy. Under the 1978 Act employees may receive payments in the event of their dismissal by reason of redundancy. There is no right to such payments where the employee unreasonably refuses an offer of re-engagement. The employer has a duty to consult union representatives when redundancies are contemplated; he must consider any representations made by the unions and give his reasons for rejecting them. The Secretary of State must be informed of any proposed large-scale redundancies. *See Cowen* v. *Haden* (1983); *Birch* v. *University of Liverpool* (1985).

NOTE: An employer must provide, on request, a written statement of reasons for dismissal. The employee may complain to a tribunal if no statement is provided, or the statement is untrue. *See* 1978 Act, s. 53.

SOME MATTERS ARISING UNDER
RECENT LEGISLATION

17. Disclosure of information. An employer has a duty, on request, to disclose to an independent union (*see* **26** below) for purposes of collective bargaining, information without which the union representatives would be, to a material extent, impeded in carrying on with such bargaining, or which it would be in accordance with good industrial relations practice that he should disclose to them for the purpose of such bargaining. *See* Employment Protection Act 1975, ss. 17–21.

18. Guarantee payments. Employees continuously employed for four weeks are entitled to guarantee payments for workless days (limited to five days in each three months). But this is not in addition to or substitution for any contractual guarantee payments. *See* Employment Act 1980, s. 14.

19. Maternity pay. Dismissal for pregnancy is considered unfair except where it means that the employee is incapable of working adequately. Where her employment continues until the beginning of the eleventh week before expected confinement, she is entitled to maternity pay (paid from the Maternity Pay Fund) and to the exercise of a right to return to her old job on no less favourable terms than if she had not been absent. Failure to permit her to return (within twenty-nine weeks of confinement) may be treated as unfair dismissal. *See* the 1978 Act, ss. 33, 56, as amended by the Employment Act 1980, ss. 11, 12.

20. Time off work. A trade union official is entitled to paid time off work in connection with his activities. A union member is entitled to unpaid time off to take part in the activities (except industrial action) of a recognised, independent union. Magistrates, members of local authorities, school governors, etc., are entitled to time off (for their public duties) which is "reasonable in all the circumstances". *See* 1978 Act, ss. 27–28; *Beal* v. *Beecham Ltd.* (1982); *Ashley* v. *Ministry of Defence* (1984).

DISCRIMINATION IN EMPLOYMENT

21. Equal Pay Act 1970. This Act applies to men and women and is concerned with pay, benefits, holidays, etc. If, for example, a woman is employed at an establishment in the U.K., the terms of her contract of employment will be deemed to include an "equality clause", if not already included. This will apply where the woman is engaged on like work with a man, or on work rated as equivalent to that of a man in the same employment. *See* also the Treaty of Rome 1957, Art. 119; *Defrenne* v. *Sabena* (1981).

22. Sex Discrimination Act 1975. This Act applies to men and women and protects them against direct and indirect discrimination arising on grounds of sex. It does not apply, for example, to a situation where being a man is a genuine occupational qualification for the job. A complaint may be made to an industrial tribunal. *See Garland* v. *B.R. Engineering Ltd.* (1982); *Brennan* v. *J. H. Dewhurst* (1984).

23. Race Relations Act 1976. Under this Act, the Commission for Racial Equality is empowered to issue non-discrimination notices and to apply for injunctions to restrain persistent discrimination in areas such as employment. *See*, e.g., *Showboat Entertainment Centre* v. *Owens* (1984).

TRADE UNIONS

24. Preliminary matters. Combinations of workers were, in earlier times, strongly disapproved of by the courts. This disapproval reached perhaps its highest level in 1834, with the transportation of six agricultural labourers, charged with administering an illegal oath to other persons, binding them not to disclose "an illegal confederacy". The judgment included the following phrase: "There are cases in which, whatever may be the intentions of the parties, the necessary effect of the act done upon the public security is of such a nature that the safety of that public does require a penal example to be made." Today, however, the trade union movement includes over half the country's workers and enjoys a considerable measure of protection at law.

25. Definition of a trade union. Under the Trade Union and Labour Relations Act 1974, s. 28(1), a "trade union" means an organisation, whether permanent or temporary, which consists wholly or mainly of workers and is an organisation whose principal purposes include regulation of relations between workers and employers or employers' associations, or consists wholly or mainly of constituent or affiliated organisations which fulfil these conditions, or representatives of such organisations. *See*, e.g., *E.E.T.P.U.* v. *The Times* (1980).

26. Independent trade unions. Under the 1974 Act, s. 30(1), an independent trade union is one which is not under the domination or control of an employer or group of employers or employers' associations, and is not liable to interference by an employer or any such group arising out of the provision of financial or material support. *See Blue Circle Staff Association* v. *Certification Officer* (1977).

27. Closed shop. This phrase refers to a condition of employment whereby employers agree to employ only union members. Under the Trade Union and Labour Relations Act 1974 closed shop agreements were made legitimate. The Act refers to them as "agreements or arrangements made by or on behalf of one or more independent trade unions and one or more employers or employers' associations relating to employees of an identifiable class". Where a closed shop is in force, it is "fair" to dismiss an employee who refuses to join the specified union, except in the case of an employee who genuinely objects on grounds of conscience or deeply-held personal convictions or has reasonable grounds for refusing to belong to a particular union, or to any union: *see* Employment Act 1980.

28. Trade disputes. Under the Trade Union and Labour Relations Act 1974, s. 29(1), as amended by the Employment Act 1982, s. 18(2), a trade dispute is defined as a dispute between workers and their employers, wholly or partly relating to: terms and conditions of employment, engagements, suspension of employment, allocation of work and other duties, discipline, union membership, negotiating machinery and facilities for union officials. Should the dispute result in a cessation of work (known as a "strike"), the law allows peaceful picketing of one's own place of work for the purpose of persuading persons to work or abstain from work: see the Employment Act 1980, s. 16(1). Those who picket *another's* place of work may lose their immunity in tort: 1980 Act, s. 16: see *Duport Steels* v. *Sirs* (1980). *See* also *British Airports Authority* v. *Ashton* (1983); *Dimbleby & Sons* v. *N.U.J.* (1984). *See* Trade Union Act 1984 (secret ballots for union elections).

PROGRESS TEST 19

1. What written terms of employment must be given to an employee? **(5)**

2. What period of notice must be given to an employee with ten years of continuous employment? **(6)**

3. Enumerate the common law duties of employers and employees. **(7, 8)**

4. What is meant by "fair" and "unfair" dismissal? **(12, 13)**

5. What are the general remedies relating to unfair dismissal? **(15)**

6. Explain "guarantee payments". **(18)**

7. What is "maternity pay"? **(19)**

8. Is a trade union official ever allowed paid time off work to attend union business? **(20)**

9. In what ways does the law attempt to prevent discrimination in employment? **(21–23)**

10. How does the law define a trade union? **(25)**

11. When is a union considered "independent"? **(26)**

12. What are the distinctive features in law of the closed shop? **(27)**

13. What is meant by a "trade dispute"? **(28)**

CHAPTER XX

Other Aspects of Law (3): Consumer Law

INTRODUCTORY MATTERS

1. The decline of caveat emptor. The widespread growth of retailing in recent years has been accompanied by an expansion of legislation intended to provide the consumer with an increased measure of statutory protection. The old common law maxim *caveat emptor* ("let the buyer beware") was for long at the basis of the buyer-seller contract so that a buyer was expected to be on his guard and to "look out for himself". In recent years the force of the maxim has declined in considerable measure; thus, for example, the consumer is now protected against the seller who applies a false trade description to goods or who unreasonably attempts to exclude or restrict liability for damage resulting from negligence in the manufacture or distribution of goods. Parliament, building on the stratum of late-nineteenth century legislation, has erected a complex structure of law designed to guard the consumer against those who would exploit his lack of knowledge or credulity.

2. Aspects of consumer legislation. The following statutes which are concerned with the buying and selling of goods or services are considered below:

  (*a*) Sale of Goods Act 1979 (*see* **3–7** below);
  (*b*) Trade Descriptions Act 1968 (*see* **8–14** below);
  (*c*) Fair Trading Act 1973 (*see* **15–17** below);
  (*d*) Consumer Credit Act 1974 (*see* **18–22** below);
  (*e*) Unfair Contract Terms Act 1977 (*see* **23–26** below);
  (*f*) Supply of Goods and Services Act 1982 (*see* **27–29** below).

SALE OF GOODS ACT 1979

3. A contract for the sale of goods. The Act defines a contract for the sale of goods as "a contract whereby the seller transfers or agrees to transfer the property in the goods to the buyer for a money consideration called the price": s. 1(1).

  (*a*) "Property in the goods" means ownership.

(b) "Goods" include all personal chattels other than choses in action (e.g. debts): s. 61.

(c) The terms of a contract for the sale of goods may be *express* (i.e. agreed by buyer and seller) or *implied* under the provisions of the Act so that they will apply automatically unless their exclusion is agreed expressly.

4. Implied terms in a contract for sale of goods under the 1979 Act. The implied terms set out below relate to *conditions* and *warranties*. A "condition" is a stipulation, the breach of which may give rise to a right to treat the contract as repudiated: *see Wickman Machine Tool Sales Ltd.* v. *Schuler* (1972). A "warranty" is an agreement with reference to goods sold which is collateral to the main purpose of the contract, the breach of which gives rise to a claim for damages, but not a right to reject the goods and treat the contract as repudiated: *see* 1979 Act, s. 62; *Wallis* v. *Pratt* (1910). The following implied terms should be noted:

(a) A condition that the seller has a right to sell the goods. *See Rowland* v. *Divall* (1923).

(b) A warranty that the buyer will enjoy "quiet possession" (i.e. uninterrupted possession of the goods). *See Microbeads AG* v. *Vinhurst Road Markings Ltd.* (1975).

(c) A condition of correspondence of the goods with description. *See Re Moore and Landauer* (1921).

(d) A condition of merchantable quality and fitness for purpose. *See Thornett and Fehr* v. *Beers Ltd.* (1919).

5. Transfer of ownership. In the case of specific goods (i.e. those identified and agreed on at the time the contract is made), ownership passes to the buyer when the parties intend it to pass: s. 17(1). Where goods are unascertained, no property passes unless and until they become ascertained: s. 16. *See The Elafi* (1982).

6. Nemo dat quod non habet: no one can give what he has not got. In general, if the seller has no title to the goods, he is unable to transfer a good title to the buyer. This rule is subject to certain exceptions, for example:

(a) *Estoppel.* Where the true owner of the goods behaves in a manner which allows the buyer to believe that the seller is the true owner, the true owner cannot deny later that the buyer has acquired good title. *See Eastern Distributors* v. *Goldring* (1957).

(b) *Sale under statutory power.* A statute may confer a power of sale so that good title is transferred to the buyer. *See*, for example, Torts (Interference with Goods) Act 1977, s. 12(3).

(c) *Sale in market overt.* Where goods are sold in market overt (i.e.

open market) according to the customs of that market, a buyer acquires good title *if* he buys in good faith and with no notice of any defect in the seller's title. (The term "market overt" has been held to apply to all shops in the City of London.) *See*, for example, *Bishopsgate Motor Finance Co.* v. *Transport Brakes Ltd.* (1949). *See* also *Reid* v. *Commissioner of Police* (1973).

(*d*) *Sale by seller in possession of the goods.* Where a person having sold goods remains in possession of them, a subsequent sale of the goods to a buyer who buys in good faith and with no notice of defect in the seller's title, passes good title to that buyer: s. 25(1).

7. Performance of the contract. It is the seller's duty to deliver the goods and the buyer's duty to accept and pay for them in accordance with the contract: s. 27. It should be noted that "delivery" is defined as "a voluntary transfer of possession from one person to another".

TRADE DESCRIPTIONS ACT 1968

8. Object of the legislation. A Parliamentary spokesman said of this Act: "Its main purpose is simply to ensure, as far as we can, that when sellers state or imply certain important facts about their goods, prices and services, what they say about them will be true." It is an offence under the Act:

(*a*) to apply a false trade description to any goods; or

(*b*) to supply or offer to supply any goods to which a false trade description is applied.

Penalties under the Act include a fine *or* imprisonment up to two years, or both.

9. A "trade description". A trade description is an indication, direct or indirect, by whatever means given, of any of the following matters with respect to goods or part of goods:

(*a*) quantity, size or gauge;

(*b*) method of manufacture, production, processing or reconditioning;

(*c*) composition;

(*d*) fitness for purpose, strength, performance;

(*e*) any physical characteristics not included above;

(*f*) testing by any person and results thereof;

(*g*) approval by any person;

(*h*) place or date of manufacture, production, processing or reconditioning;

(*i*) person by whom manufactured, produced, processed or reconditioned;

(*j*) other history, including previous ownership or use: s. 2(1).

10. A "false" trade description. A false trade description is a trade description which is false to a material degree: s. 3. A trade description which though not false, is misleading, is deemed to be a false trade description.

11. "Applying" a trade description. Under s. 4, a person is considered to "apply" a description to goods if he affixes or annexes it or in any manner marks it on or incorporates it with the goods themselves or anything in, on or with which the goods are supplied, or places the goods in, on or with anything which the description has been affixed or annexed to, or uses the description in any manner likely to be taken as referring to the goods.

12. Prices. Under s. 11, if a person gives a false indication to the effect that the price at which goods are offered is equal to or less than a recommended price or the price at which the goods of the same description were previously offered by him, is less than such a price by a specified amount, he is guilty of an offence. *See Westminster C.C.* v. *Ray Alan (Manshops)* (1982).

13. Services. The Act covers goods and services. Under s. 14, it is an offence for a person in the course of a trade or business to make a statement which he knows to be false, or recklessly to make a statement which is false, as to matters concerning:

(*a*) the provision of services, accommodation or facilities;

(*b*) the nature of services, accommodation or facilities;

(*c*) the location or amenities of accommodation.

See Dixons v. *Roberts* (1984); *Wings* v. *Ellis* (1984).

14. Defences. Under s. 24 it is a defence for a person charged under the Act to prove:

(*a*) that the commission of the offence was due to a mistake or to reliance on information supplied to him or to the act or default of any other person, to an accident or to some other cause beyond his control; *and*

(*b*) that he took all reasonable precautions and exercised all due diligence to avoid the commission of such an offence by himself or any person under his control. *See Naish* v. *Gore* (1971); *Stainthorpe* v. *Bailey* (1980).

NOTE: The Trade Descriptions Act 1972 makes it an offence for a person in the course of a business to supply imported goods which have a clearly visible name or mark which is, or might be taken as, a U.K. name or mark unless they bear an indication of the country of manufacture.

FAIR TRADING ACT 1973

15. "Fair trading". The concept of fair trading is given expression in the 1973 Act through the powers of the Director-General of Fair Trading. He has the duty of keeping under review the carrying on of commercial activities which relate "to goods or to services supplied to or for consumers in the U.K.". He collects information relating to practices "which may adversely affect the economic interest of consumers in the U.K.".

16. Unfair consumer trade practices. The Director-General may refer to the Consumer Protection Advisory Committee for its consideration "any practice which is for the time being carried on in connection with the supply of goods or services to or for consumers". Such a practice must relate to:

(*a*) the terms or conditions on or subject to which goods or services are supplied;

(*b*) the manner in which those terms are communicated;

(*c*) the promotion or methods of salesmanship relating to goods and services;

(*d*) the manner in which goods are packaged;

(*e*) methods of demanding or securing payment for goods or services supplied.

17. Recommendations by the Director-General. Where it appears to the Director-General that a consumer trade practice should be curbed, he may recommend such a course of action to the Secretary of State who may issue an appropriate statutory instrument. (Few such instruments have been issued; they include instruments relating to prepayment in mail order transactions, sale of goods without revealing that they are being sold in the course of a business and practices relating to advertising VAT-exclusive prices or charges.) Under s. 17 a practice can be "considered" by the Director-General if it is likely to have the following effects:

(*a*) misleading consumers as to their rights and obligations;

(*b*) misleading or confusing consumers in connection with transactions;

(*c*) subjecting consumers to undue pressure to enter into transactions;

(*d*) causing terms or conditions on or subject to which consumers enter into relevant consumer transactions to be so adverse to them as to be inequitable.

CONSUMER CREDIT ACT 1974

18. Objects of the Act. The 1974 Act has two major objects:

(*a*) the provision of a uniform system of statutory control relating to the granting of "credit" (i.e. cash loans and other forms of financial accommodation;

(*b*) the protection of the interests of consumers by the establishing of a system of licences granted to persons offering credit facilities.

19. "Regulated agreements". The 1974 Act relates to *regulated agreements*. These are as follows:

(*a*) *Consumer credit agreements*, i.e. personal credit agreements under the terms of which the creditor provides the debtor with credit not exceeding an amount stated in the Act.

(*b*) *Consumer hire agreements*, i.e. bailments of goods for more than three months, for not more than an amount stated in the Act, and which are not the subject of hire-purchase agreements.

(*c*) *Credit token agreements*, i.e. those involving cards, stamps, etc., given to an individual by a person carrying on a consumer credit business.

20. Entry into a regulated agreement. Under s. 55, before an agreement is made, the debtor must be given such information as is required by any regulations made by the Secretary of State. Under s. 61, the agreement must be in writing, must be signed by the debtor and by, or on behalf of, all other parties.

21. Protected goods. Goods are deemed "protected goods" under s. 90 of the Act when they are the subject of a regulated hire-purchase agreement or conditional sale agreement *and*:

(*a*) the debtor has paid or tendered one-third or more of the total price of the goods;

(*b*) the property in the goods remains in the creditor;

(*c*) the debtor has not terminated the agreement.

In these circumstances the goods may be recovered *only by court order*, unless the debtor has agreed to surrender them. *See Bentinck Ltd.* v. *Cromwell Engineering Co.* (1971).

22. Licensing. The Act requires the issue of licences to persons wishing to provide finance under regulated agreements. "Standard" licences are issued to trading or financial entities. "Group" licences may be issued to groups of persons. A licence may be required also by persons carrying on any "ancillary credit business" (i.e. one relating to credit-brokerage, debt-adjusting, debt-counselling, debt-collecting or the operations of a credit reference agency). The

Director-General of Fair Trading may vary, suspend or revoke licences.

UNFAIR CONTRACT TERMS ACT 1977

23. Object of the Act. This Act is intended to impose limits on the extent to which civil liability for breach of contract, or for negligence or other breach of duty, can be avoided by means of terms in contracts. The Act applies to contracts for the sale of goods and of hire-purchase, other contracts under which possession or ownership of goods passes, and contracts for the supply of goods or services to which the Supply of Goods and Services Act 1982 applies (*see* **27** below). *See Walker* v. *Boyle* (1982); *George Mitchell* v. *Finney Lock Seeds* (1983); *Ailsa Craig Fishing Co.* v. *Malvern Fishing Co.* (1983).

24. Negligence liability. A person cannot by reference to any contract term or to a notice given exclude or restrict his liability for death or personal injury resulting from negligence. In the case of other loss or damage a person cannot so exclude or restrict his liability for negligence except in so far as the term or notice satisfies the requirement of reasonableness: s. 2.

25. Unreasonable indemnity clauses. A person dealing as a consumer cannot by reference to any contract term be made to indemnify another person (whether a party to the contract or not) in respect of liability that may be incurred by the other for negligence or breach of contract, except in so far as the contract term satisfies the requirement of reasonableness: s. 4. *See Phillips Products* v. *Hylands* (1984).

26. "Dealing as consumer". A party to a contract "deals as consumer" in relation to another party if he neither makes the contract in the course of a business nor holds himself out as doing so; and the other party does make the contract in the course of a business; and, in the case of a contract governed by the law of sale of goods or hire-purchase, the goods are of a type ordinarily supplied for private use or consumption: s. 12.

SUPPLY OF GOODS AND SERVICES ACT 1982

27. Object of the Act. The 1982 Act gives rights concerning title, description and quality of goods, similar to those arising under the Sale of Goods Act 1979 (*see* **3–7** above), to parties to contracts which are neither contracts for the sale of goods nor hire-purchase. Further, the Act implies certain terms in contracts where one party has agreed to carry out services. (But it has no application to contracts of employment or apprenticeship.)

28. Contracts for transfer of property in goods. Terms are implied concerning freedom from charges or encumbrances, quiet possession of the goods (s. 2), correspondence of goods with description (s. 3), merchantable quality and fitness for purpose (s. 4), and samples (s. 5).

29. Contracts for services. The Act implies terms relating to the carrying out of the service with reasonable care and skill (s. 13), the carrying out of the service within a reasonable time (s. 14), and the paying of a reasonable charge by the customer where none is stated in the contract (s. 15). What is a "reasonable time" or a "reasonable charge" is a question of fact (ss. 14, 15).

PROGRESS TEST 20

1. Explain *caveat emptor*. **(1)**
2. What is a "contract for the sale of goods"? **(3)**
3. Explain the phrase "market overt". **(6)**
4. Outline the main provisions of the Trade Descriptions Act 1968. **(8–14)**
5. Comment on the powers of the Director-General of Fair Trading under the Fair Trading Act 1973. **(15–17)**
6. What are "protected goods" under the Consumer Credit Act 1974? **(21)**
7. What is the effect of the Unfair Contract Terms Act 1977 upon unreasonable indemnity clauses? **(25)**
8. What is the object of the Supply of Goods and Services Act 1982? **(27)**

Selected Reading List

In all cases only the most recent editions should be used.

English Legal System:

English Legal System: Eddey (Sweet and Maxwell)
English Legal System: Kiralfy (Sweet and Maxwell)
English Legal System: Walker (Butterworths)
The Modern English Legal System: Smith and Bailey (Sweet and Maxwell)

General Principles of Law:

General Principles of Law: Metcalfe (Cassell)
General Principles of Law: Newton (Sweet and Maxwell)
Introduction to English Law: James (Butterworths)
English Law: Smith and Keenan (Pitman)

British Constitution:

British Constitution: Jennings (C.U.P.)
The British Constitution: Bagehot (O.U.P.)
Parliament: Jennings (C.U.P.)
Constitutional Law: Wade and Phillips (Longman)

The Courts:

The Courts of Law: Walker (David and Charles)
Criminal Procedure: Hampton (Sweet and Maxwell)
The Criminal Court in Action: Barnard (Butterworths)
The Civil Court in Action: Barnard (Butterworths)

Evidence:

Evidence: Cross (Butterworths)
Outline of the Law of Evidence: Cross and Wilkins (Butterworths)
Phipson's Manual of the Law of Evidence: Elliot (Sweet and Maxwell)

Criminal Law:

Criminal Law: Smith and Hogan (Butterworths)

Criminal Law: Seago (Sweet and Maxwell)
Textbook of Criminal Law: Williams (Stevens)

Contract:

Law of Contract: Cheshire and Fifoot (Butterworths)
Law of Contract: Treitel (Sweet and Maxwell)
Contract: Davies (Sweet and Maxwell)

Torts:

Law of Torts: Salmond (Sweet and Maxwell)
Law of Torts: Street (Butterworths)
Tort: Baker (Sweet and Maxwell)

Land Law:

Modern Law of Real Property: Cheshire (Butterworths)
Manual of the Law of Real Property: Megarry (Stevens)
Land Law: Dalton (Oyez)

Trusts:

Law of Trusts: Keeton (Pitman)
Modern Law of Trusts: Parker and Mellows (Sweet and Maxwell)
Law of Trusts: Riddall (Butterworths)

Family Law:

Family Law: Bromley (Butterworths)
Family Law: Levin (Sweet and Maxwell)
Principles of Family Law: Cretney (Sweet and Maxwell)

Employment Law:

Employment Law: Hepple and O'Higgins (Sweet and Maxwell)
Principles of Labour Law: Rideout (Sweet and Maxwell)
Labour Law: Smith and Wood (Sweet and Maxwell)

General Reading:

Learning the Law: Williams (Stevens)
Introduction to Legal Method: Farrar (Sweet and Maxwell)
The Idea of Law: Lloyd (Penguin)
Introduction to Law: Rutherford, Todd and Woodley (Sweet and Maxwell)
The Law Machine: Berlins and Dyer (Penguin)
The English Legal Process: Ingman (Financial Training)

NOTE: The Macdonald & Evans series of HANDBOOKS contains titles relating to all the above sections.

Examination Technique

1. Elementary examinations in principles of law. The object of elementary examinations in law, such as those set at "O" and "A" levels, is, in general, the testing of a candidate's comprehension of basic legal principles and his ability to apply those principles to simple problems.

2. Types of questions set. Three general types of question tend to appear in elementary papers, but it must be emphasised that there is often considerable overlap.

(*a*) *The purely factual question:*

(*i*) Explain how European Community law affects English law.

(*ii*) What is meant by a trust? Outline the differences between a private and a public trust.

(*b*) *The discussion question:*

(*i*) Is the principle of separation of powers of any significance today in the United Kingdom?

(*ii*) "The real advantage of ownership is that you can do as you wish with your property." Consider this statement in relation to the ownership of a piano and a plot of land.

(*c*) *The problem question:*

(*i*) Albert and his son, Bill, aged thirteen, enter a shop intending to steal goods. Albert picks up a watch and hands it to Bill who puts it in his pocket. Later that day Albert phones Charles and arranges to sell the watch to him. Consider the criminal liability, if any, of Albert, Bill and Charles.

(*ii*) John, a professional guitarist, orders six sets of guitar strings from a music retailer. After delivery, John, who is aged seventeen, refuses to pay. Advise the retailer.

3. The purely factual question. Answers to questions of this type must be factual, comprehensive, relevant and always precise. Thus, question **2**(*a*) (*ii*) above calls for a precise definition of a trust. Examples and illustrations will help. The second part of the question demands an answer based on the enumeration in clear terms of the principal differences between the two types of trust.

4. The discussion question. A basis of facts, upon which is built a relevant discussion, is required in answer to this type of question.

Consider question 2(*b*) (*i*). An answer to this question necessitates, initially, a precise explanation of separation of powers, followed by illustrations of the principle in practice today. The word "significance" in the question must not be overlooked, so that an answer ought to indicate how important the candidate considers the principle to be in our legal system.

5. The problem question. This type of question calls for an answer based on a knowledge of legal principles and the capacity to apply it to the problem set out in the data. Consider question 2(*c*) (*i*) above. Initially, it is necessary to identify the principles underlying the problem. In this case it is clearly a matter relating to stealing. How is stealing defined by statute? Do the actions of Albert and Bill come within that definition? Is Bill's age of any relevance to his criminal liability? What of Charles' actions? Does he know that the watch is stolen? Ought he to know? Do his actions constitute the offence of "handling" under the Theft Act 1968?

6. In the examination room. The following points should be noted carefully:

(*a*) *Read the questions very carefully indeed*, noting those you intend to answer.

(*b*) *Plan your use of available time*, allocating it equally to all the questions to be answered and ensuring that you allow time for swift revision and correction of your answers before the paper is handed in.

(*c*) *Plan in outline each question before writing your answer*. This is *never* time wasted. Check the pattern of your answer, ensuring that legal principles are stated correctly, that illustrations are relevant and that appropriate conclusions are drawn. Aim at *precision, clarity and coherence*. Avoid irrelevance, "padding out" of answers (which never gains marks) and guessing. Aim to show the examiner that you have acquired a basic sense of "legal thinking", i.e. that you have understood the importance of *analysing* legal problems before suggesting answers to them.

Test Papers

Answer any *five* questions from each of the three test papers.
Time allowed for each paper: two hours.

PAPER I

1. "No law, no civilisation." Discuss.
2. What is the importance of precedent in English law?
3. Outline some of the differences in meaning attached to "owner-ship" and "possession".
4. What is the importance in English law of Parliamentary supremacy?
5. John brings an action against William who has failed to pay for goods to the value of £10,000 which have been delivered to him. Outline the course of the action.
6. What types of evidence may be given in court?
7. X shoots Y after a violent quarrel. X is charged with Y's murder and pleads that he was provoked by Y's referring to him as "a bully and a thief". Discuss.
8. Can an agreement be rendered void if one of the parties has not really understood the terms of the document he was signing?
9. What are the general defences to an action for defamation?
10. In what ways does the law protect the rights of consumers?

PAPER II

1. "Law is the state's rules by which our lives are governed." Discuss.
2. How important is delegated legislation today?
3. What judicial functions are exercised by the House of Lords?
4. "The criminal law is a sword and a shield." Discuss.
5. "Every convicted person has a right of appeal." Discuss.
6. In what ways has English law reacted to the evils arising from misuse of drugs?
7. What remedies are available to a party injured by breach of contract?

8. "A man may do with his land as he wishes." How true is this statement?

9. Why are charitable trusts of importance?

10. "Divorce is now a very simple matter." Discuss.

PAPER III

1. "The rock upon which English law rests is the common law." Explain the meaning of this statement.

2. "One man's right is another man's duty." Discuss.

3. Would it be advantageous if our constitution were to be set down in written form?

4. What is the importance of the division of the English legal profession into barristers and solicitors?

5. What standard of proof is required in a case where X alleges a breach of contract by Y?

6. How does the criminal law deal with an allegation that A struck B after an argument?

7. "*Consensus ad idem* is at the basis of every contract." Discuss.

8. What are the essential features of a mortgage?

9. How does the law seek to supervise the process of adoption?

10. What rights in law have been granted to trade unions?

Index